Leslie Linsley's
Night Before Christmas Craft Book

Also by Leslie Linsley

Leslie Linsley's Night Before Christmas Craft Book

Design and photography by Jon Aron

St. Martin's/Marek

Design by Jon Aron

Library of Congress Cataloging in Publication Data
Linsley, Leslie.
    The Night before Christmas craft book.
    1. Christmas decorations.   2. Handicraft.
3. Gifts.   I. Title.
TT900.C4L57   1984   745.594′1   84-13256
ISBN 0-312-57277-8

First Edition
10 9 8 7 6 5 4 3 2 1

I would like to acknowledge the excellent craftwork done by Robby Aron in the needlework and cross-stitch sections, and also her contribution to the calligraphy projects.

Contents

Leslie Linsley's
Night Before Christmas Craft Book

Introduction

"Twas the night before Christmas" . . . and you suddenly realize that you forgot to get Aunt Helen a present. Or, you've been invited to drop by for a visit next door and you need a small gift. Christmas time brings so many pressures that it's easy to get bogged down. And much as we'd like to do everything there simply isn't enough time.

I am a full-time working mother. My career involves designing and making craft projects and I am always creating new ideas and products for books, magazines, and companies. I rarely have time to make things just for the fun of it. At Christmas time this is particularly frustrating. It's a time of year when even the busiest person is bitten by the creative bug. And there are so many ways to express yourself—from the tiniest felt tree ornament to a lovingly hand-knit afghan. Our homes cry out for personal decorations to add sparkle and joy to the holiday spirit.

So it seems fitting that we not give up the rewards of a handmade Christmas but find a way to fit crafting into our busy schedules. It occurred to me that a last-minute gift, decoration, or ornament needn't look any less wonderful than one that takes days or even weeks to create. And so, along with my designer husband, Jon Aron, I've used the "last-minute" theme to create projects that can be made quickly and easily from readily available materials. In fact, the last chapter is devoted entirely to throwaway treasures—you don't even have to leave your home to buy materials. The fabric section utilizes scraps from the sewing basket, and the knit items can be made from leftover yarns.

Not everything in this book is exactly last minute. There are quite a few projects that require a full weekend but the results will prove well worth the time as they have lasting qualities. The cross-stitch poinsettia tray on page 49, for example, will be used over and over again. Each Christmas will remind you of Christmases past.

Two years ago I wrote a book called *Christmas Ornaments and Stockings*. It was very popular and last year the publisher reissued it in paperback so that more people could afford to buy it. Many of the projects were appealing enough to provoke some lovely letters telling me which crafting techniques were most enjoyable. A few people suggested ideas for another book. Almost everyone expressed the fact that they wished they had more time for these activities. Well, now I have a chance to solve this problem and at the same time to incorporate some of the most popular techniques for making smaller items.

Gift tags were among the most frequent requests and I think you'll find our country style tags the simplest ever. Calligraphy is another area of interest, but a very simplified lesson was needed. Now you can send all your Christmas cards out with beautifully scripted hand lettering that won't take you much time to learn.

I think you'll find a selection of projects to your liking even if you've never done any craftwork before. From wood appliqué to counted cross-stitch, from knitting to needlepoint, the variety of techniques will make Christmas crafting more fun than ever before. And I think the most fun will be in giving these quick and easy gifts that really don't look it.

General crafting how-to's

All your favorite crafting techniques are used to create a variety of projects for last-minute gift giving. While each item features specific step by step directions, there are some general tips and how-to's that pertain to all the projects. These can be most helpful, especially when you are working on several items at once.

The following general directions will tell you the best ways to do various steps. They'll also help you prepare the materials needed in the most efficient way.

Enlarging designs and patterns

Although most of the projects have been designed and presented full-size, occasionally it is necessary to enlarge a design. In such cases I have provided a grid and indicated the size each square represents. Usually one square equals 1 inch. You then transfer or copy the design to paper marked off with 1-inch squares. You can make your own graph paper or buy a pad in an art supply store.

Transferring designs and patterns

You can transfer most of the designs from this book to another surface such as fabric or a box. Simply retrace the design on the back of the paper. Place this over the object and rub the pencil over the outlines. Remove the tracing and go over the design so you can see it more clearly on the object.

Cutting out patterns

Take the time to determine how you will place each pattern piece on the fabric to get the most from your material. This is especially important when making multiples. For example, when making ornaments in quantity first choose a variety of fabrics so that each will look different. Decide how many of each you want and cut out several layers of fabric using the one pattern piece. The number of layers to be cut at one time will depend on the type of fabric used. If you're using a solid or overall print, placement isn't a problem. When using stripes or a one-way print, take the extra care to cut pieces in the right direction.

After all the pieces are cut out, they must be individually marked.

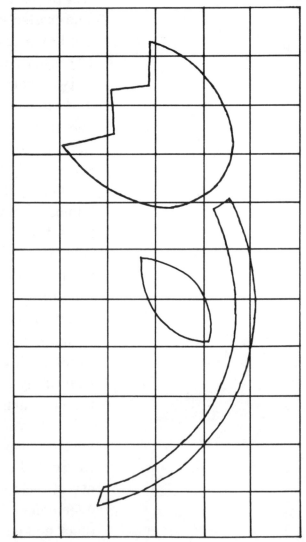

Grid method of enlarging

Sewing

Sewing pattern pieces in the right sequence makes a big difference in time and efficiency.

Plan thread colors so that all stitching with one color can be done before changing spool and bobbin.

If you're working in quantity, do all the same steps on all ornaments at one time rather than completing one and starting the next. However, sometimes I do like to complete the first one to have a sample to work from.

Any hand or lap work such as stuffing and finishing openings should be done at one time. I like to save these finishing details to do while watching TV or just relaxing.

When working on the cross-stitch projects (see page 43), draw the outlines of the pattern on the fabric. Cross-stitch each item before cutting it out and finishing. If you have a cut piece, seal the edges with masking tape while working with it. This prevents the edges from raveling.

Trimmings add uniqueness and give the item a finished look. If you're working on several projects, do all trimming last. This is an enjoyable and creative activity so save leftover scraps of lace, ribbons, buttons, etc., for the added touches.

Patchwork and appliqué

Patchwork and appliqué are traditional methods for making quilts. Patchwork is the sewing together of fabric pieces to create an entire design. Sometimes the shapes form a geometric block. The blocks are then sewn together to make up a completed quilt. Although the patchwork projects are designed for fast crafting, the techniques can be applied to larger projects.

Appliqué is the technique of creating a design by cutting a shape from one fabric and stitching it to a contrasting fabric backing. When applying one fabric to another you can use a matching thread or a contrasting one to define the appliquéd shapes. Pin or baste the shapes in place on the fabric. You can use an invisible hemming stitch or overcast the raw edges with embroidery floss. Or, you can use a narrow, short zigzag stitch all around the appliqué.

General crafting materials

I am often asked which materials are best for certain crafting techniques and which brands I recommend. While I seldom endorse any one product, I have found over the years that some products do work better than others. Also, readers often can't find certain material without a brand name. For example, you might try to find an even-weave fabric for cross-stitch in notions stores. It's much easier, however, to ask for Aida or Hardanger in a needlepoint shop. So where it is helpful I have mentioned products by name.

The following is general information and advice about materials.

Paint

Acrylic paint is recommended for painting the stenciled boxes and decoupage bottles. You can buy it in small tubes in every color imaginable. It washes off hands and brushes; however, it is permanent on fabric. This makes it ideal for fabric stenciling and many other craft projects as well.

The brands most readily available are Liquitex and Grumbacher. Always buy a tube of white to mix with the colors as even the pastels are usually too bright. A drop of color goes a long way.

Krylon spray paint is available in all hardware stores and this is what I used on the spray-painted projects. The colors, more limited than the acrylic colors, are very bright.

Stencils

In the chapter on stenciling you'll find the best techniques to use. The many stencil kits on the market include precut designs. This takes the hard part out of stenciling (cutting the stencils), but limits your designs to what is commercially available. Once you learn to cut a stencil yourself, the design possibilities are limitless.

Go to a good art supply store for brushes, stencil paper, and paints. The better the brush, the easier it will be to create perfect stencils. Brushes come in various sizes for different projects and I recommend having one brush for each color.

Acetate is the preferred paper, but you can also use oak tag, manila folders, or Mylar to cut a stencil.

Fabrics

Almost any fabric can be used for the projects in this book; however, some are easier to work with for different crafting techniques.

Many Christmas craft projects are made with felt because it comes in a variety of colors and you can buy small pieces in the five-and-ten. Felt won't fray and therefore doesn't have to be hemmed.

Even-weave fabric such as Aida and Hardanger is used for cross-stitch. Since it is expensive, I've designed only small projects using this material. Small-checked gingham is a good background for cross-stitch and I've used large-grid fabric from International Printworks for larger, quicker projects. (See the mail-order source list on page 160 for grid fabric in all colors.)

Muslin is a good, inexpensive backing material and is often used for country pillows such as the one on page 106. It is also a good background for stenciling. Muslin comes 60-inches wide and sells for approximately $3.00 a yard.

Plastic canvas is used whenever possible rather than regular needlepoint canvas, which is sold by the yard. The plastic type is cheaper, comes in precut shapes, and needs no blocking.

Polished cotton, satin, and velvet will give any of the projects an elegant look. Small overall prints like calico are good choices for small projects.

Stacy's Stitch Witchery is used to fuse two pieces of fabric together, as with appliqué (see page 118). You can buy it in strips, small packages, or by the yard. You will find it invaluable for tacking down ribbon trim, when you're in a rush and don't want to do a lot of sewing, for tacking hems, and for a million other little projects.

Stacy makes another product to aid the home sewer as well: Trace Erase is used to embroider on fabric and yarn. The project on page 134 is an example of how easy it is to have perfect embroidery on a yarn surface.

Basic stitches

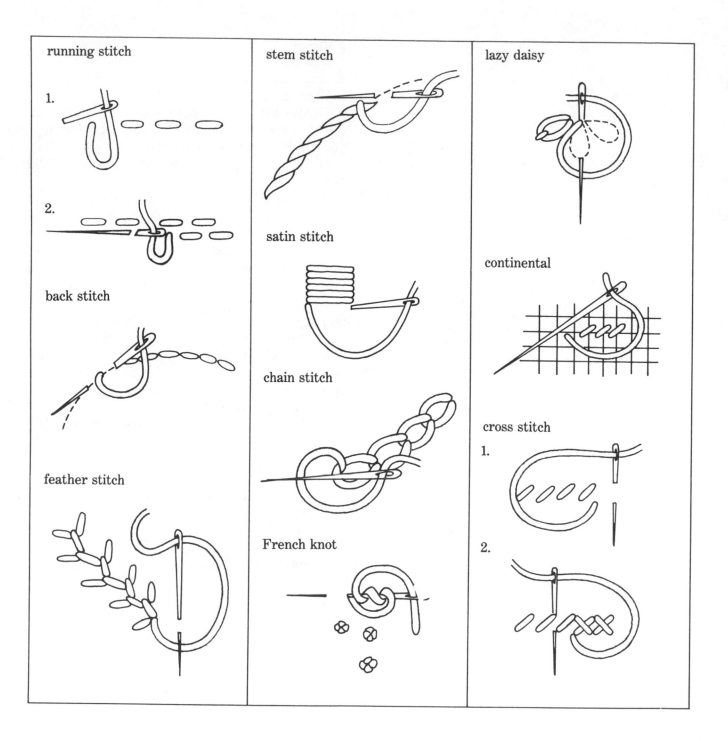

running stitch

1.

2.

back stitch

feather stitch

stem stitch

satin stitch

chain stitch

French knot

lazy daisy

continental

cross stitch

1.

2.

Needlepoint

Most of the needlepoint projects are small enough to be made in an evening. Plastic canvas has made needlepoint easier than it used to be because it can be cut into shapes and no blocking is necessary.

Plastic canvas comes in 11 × 14–inch sheets and is available in 5-, 7-, and 10-count mesh. Most five and tens also sell it prepackaged with a dozen round, square, or diamond shapes.

Although plastic canvas is flexible it isn't soft like regular cloth canvas. Therefore it isn't the best material for all projects. The eyeglass case on page 36, for example, is made with regular canvas. The teddy bear ornament on page 41 is made with plastic canvas as are such items as coasters and frames where the sturdiness of the material is an advantage.

It is easiest to find white, but the plastic sheets and shapes also come in red and green. With the colored canvas you can do a design without having to fill in the background.

Almost all the needlepoint projects are worked with Persian-type yarn that comes in small 12½-yard skeins. You can buy several skeins in the colors needed for each project. This yarn is acrylic and washable. You might prefer 100% wool in the 3-ply weight for the eyeglass case or change purse as it looks better and lacks the sheen of acrylic.

When purchasing yarn, be sure to get enough of each color. Dye lots differ and it's sometimes hard to match colors exactly.

To add to the ease of doing these items, they are all worked with the popular Continental stitch. All projects are charted for placement of stitches and each color is indicated on the chart.

Finish the design before cutting out the shape and leave at least one row of unworked canvas around the design when cutting out. In this way you can bind around the design for a finished edge; you will also have a seam allowance if needed. Sometimes a double strand of yarn finishes the edges more completely.

Needles: An embroidery needle has a blunt point and comes in various sizes. A #17–18 needle is the most commonly used on the popular 10- and 12-count meshes.

Friendship frame

Use this heart theme to create a needlepoint frame for your favorite 3 × 5–inch snapshot. It is made with plastic canvas and a small amount of red and white yarn. This is a good project to make with leftovers.

Materials: 10-count 6 × 8–inch plastic canvas; 12½-yard skeins of 1–2–3 ply Persian-type yarn—1 each of red and white; needle; cardboard for backing; glue.

Directions

Leaving a couple of rows on either edge, locate one corner to begin and follow the chart to make one row of white in the Continental stitch (see stitch guide on page 18) all around.

Continue to follow chart for placement of stitches and colors to create heart patterns. Finish with last row around center opening (not yet cut) in white.

Cut center rectangle and trim around outside edges. Bind off around inside and outside edges with red yarn.

No blocking is necessary with plastic canvas. Cut cardboard backing to fit back of frame. Position frame over snapshot and tape on back.

Spread white glue on backing and attach to back of framed photograph. Set aside to dry.

Trace pattern for photo stand and transfer to heavy cardboard such as poster or shirt board. Cut and bend along line indicated. Glue to center back of photo so it stands correctly.

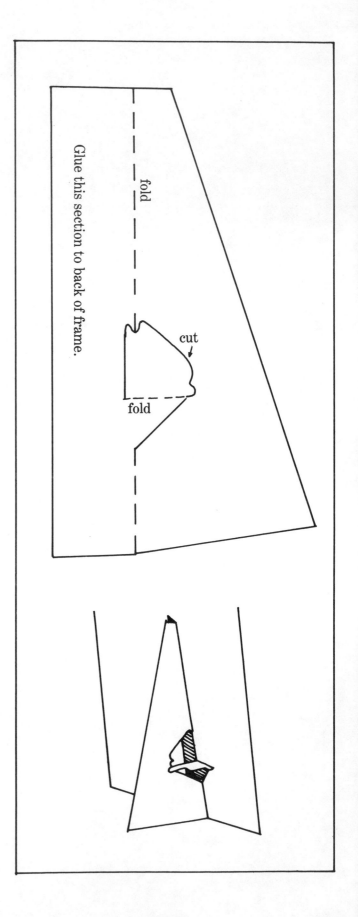

Friendship frame

⊠ red

☐ white

It's always a treat to bring out accessories that are used only at Christmas time. They cheer up the house and make it special when entertaining. So while these coasters probably won't be used at any other time of the year, they are very cheery for that special time. Choose alphabet letters from pages 24 and 25 and make one with a friend's first initial and another with the last.

Materials: 10-count plastic canvas, 4½-inch square (if precut); 1–2–3 ply Persian-type yarn— 1 skein each of red and green, 2 skeins white; needle; red or green felt for backing; glue.

Directions

Use the Continental stitch and follow the chart for placement of colors. When finished, bind off with a row of green worked around edge and into last row worked with green.

Cut a square of felt for back of each coaster and glue or stitch in place.

☐ white

☒ red

⊡ green

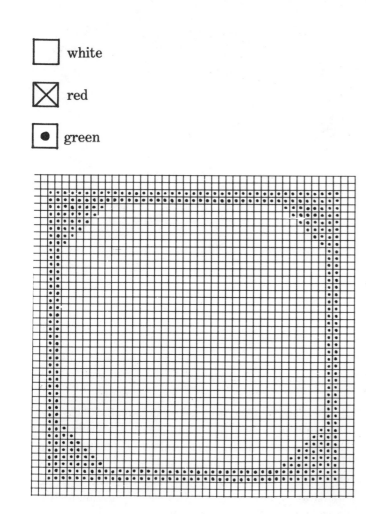

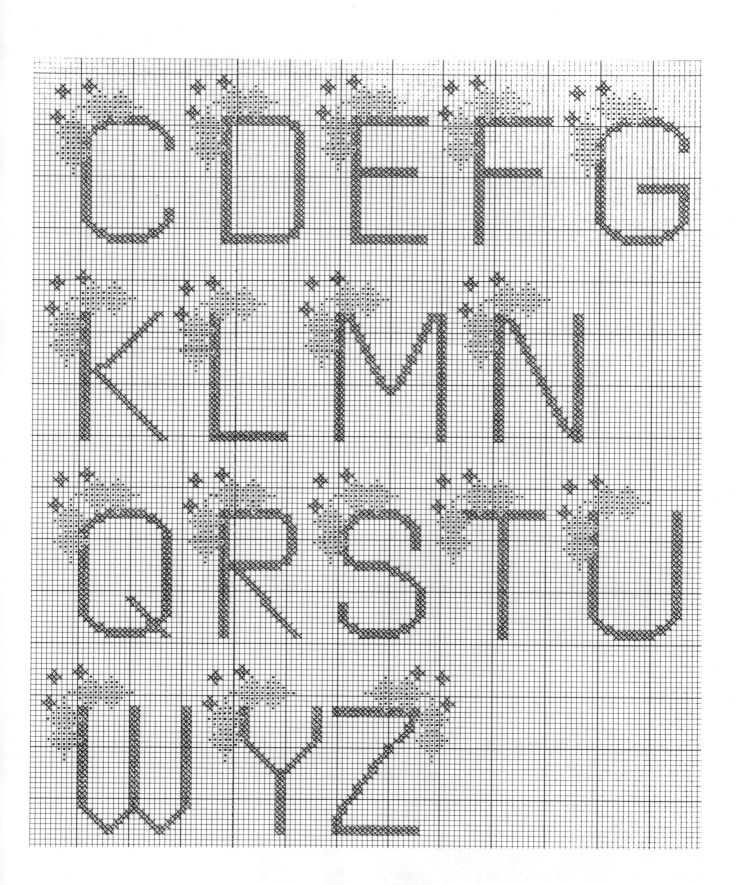

Basket wreath

Needlepoint a small wreath to place on a basket for a decorative centerpiece or for holding Christmas cards. You could also attach the wreath to the front door. The completed project is 6 × 7 inches.

Materials: 10-count plastic canvas; 1–2–3 ply Persian-type yarn—1 skein each of red, royal blue, light green, gold, pink, light blue, white, light yellow, and dark green and 2 skeins navy blue; needle; felt for backing and glue (if desired).

Directions

Work on a full sheet of plastic canvas and follow the chart for placement of colors and stitches. Use the Continental stitch throughout.

When finished, cut around design and bind off with navy blue for the wreath and red for the bow. Cut out center area and bind off with navy blue yarn.

If desired, cut a piece of felt to fit back of wreath and glue in place.

Color key for chart on page 28

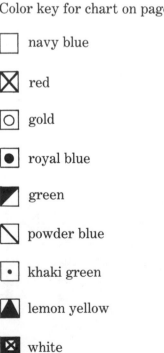

☐ navy blue

☒ red

⊡ gold

⦿ royal blue

◪ green

◹ powder blue

⊡ khaki green

▲ lemon yellow

⊠ white

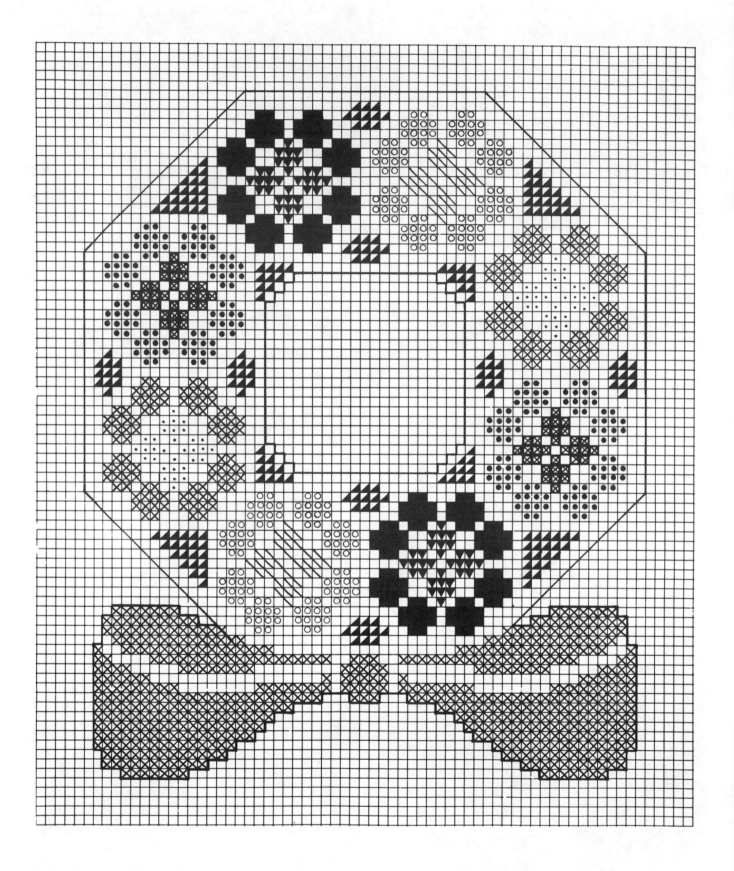

Use the alphabet on opposite page and personalize a gift for your best friends and relatives. The monogrammed coaster on page 23 is strictly for Christmas-time use. This design can be used at holiday time and all year round as well. If you want to jazz it up for Christmas use red and green colors rather than the red and blue used here.

Materials: 10-count plastic canvas, 4½-inch square; 1–2–3 ply Persian-type yarn—1 skein each of blue and white, 2 skeins red; needle; red felt for backing; glue (optional).

Directions

Follow the chart for placement of stitches and colors. Work in the Continental stitch. Bind around coaster with red yarn worked into white row (last row worked).

To finish, cut piece of red felt to fit back and glue or stitch to coaster.

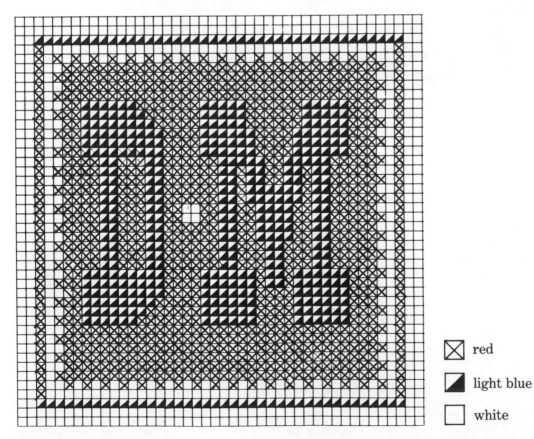

⊠ red

◪ light blue

☐ white

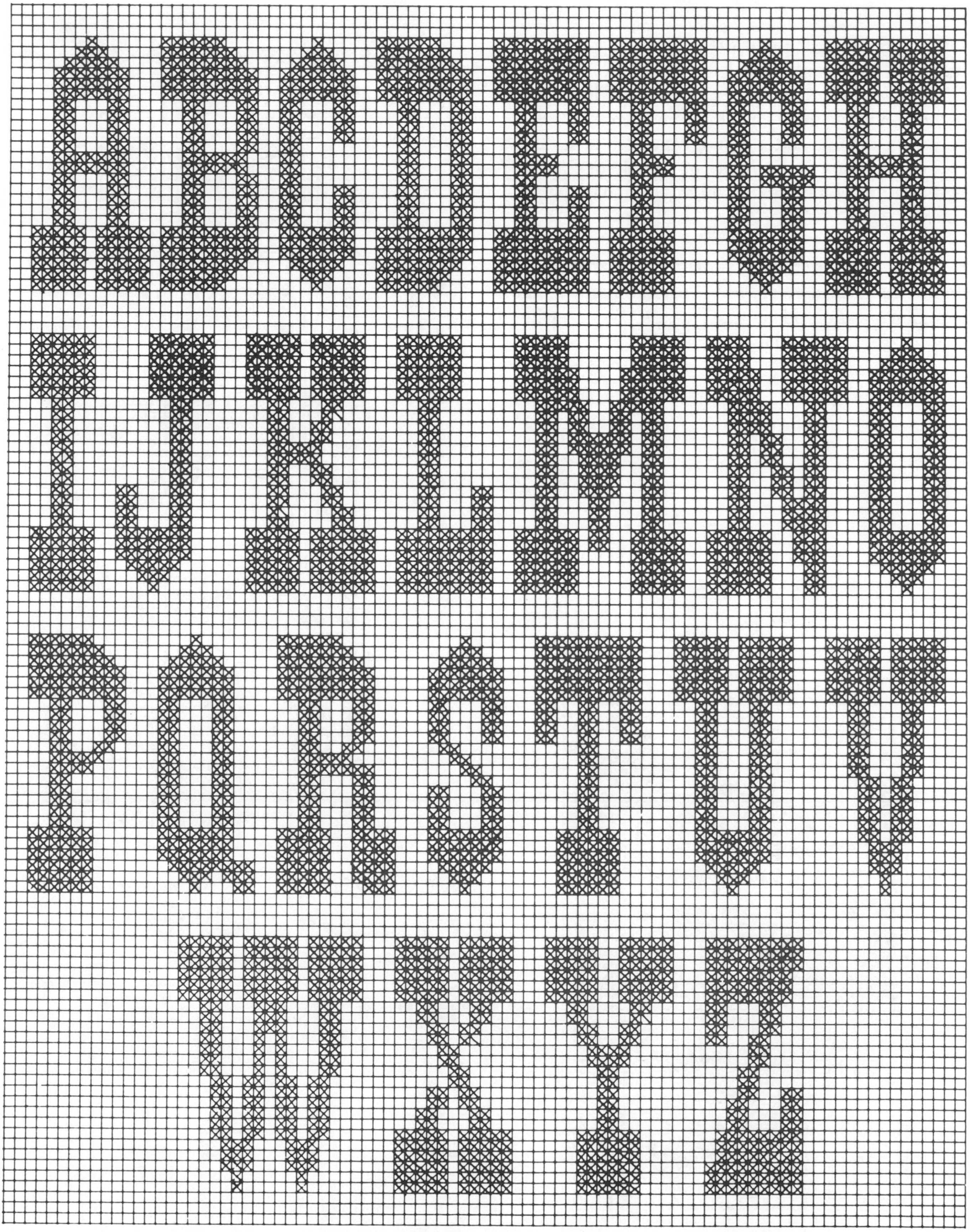

Bookmarks

Bookmarks are quick little projects that I've designed to be whimsical for a change of pace. There is a bee and flower on one, a boat and anchor on another, a cat and mouse that you can make for a child, and a monogram with hearts.

Give someone you care about a book for Christmas and add your handmade gift for that special touch.

Materials for each bookmark: Small amount of 10-count plastic canvas; 1–2–3 ply Persian yarn in the colors indicated on each chart; ¼-inch-wide satin ribbon, 10 inches long; needle.

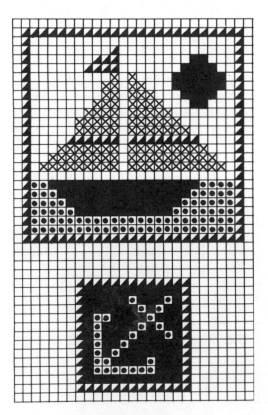

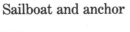

Sailboat and anchor

☐ light blue

■ yellow

⊠ white

◤ red

⊙ medium blue

Monogram bookmark

⊠ wine red

⊡ pink

☐ white

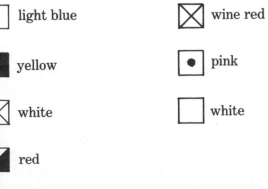

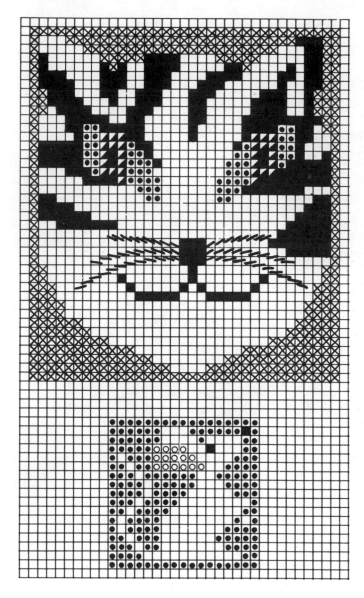

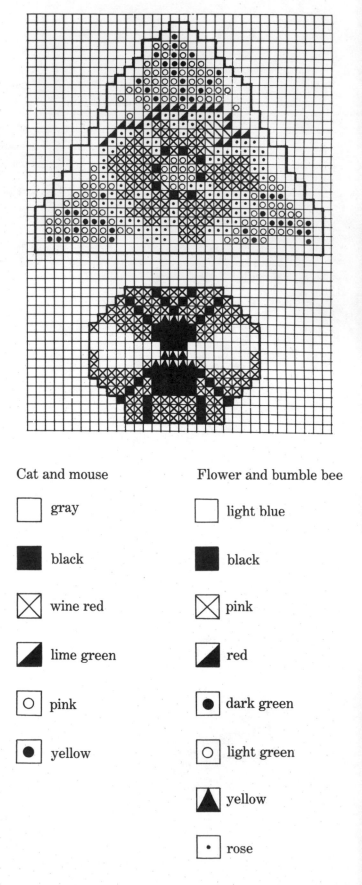

Cat and mouse

☐ gray

■ black

⊠ wine red

◩ lime green

◉ pink

⦿ yellow

Flower and bumble bee

☐ light blue

■ black

⊠ pink

◩ red

⦿ dark green

◉ light green

◣ yellow

⊡ rose

Directions

The Continental stitch is used for all projects. Start with a big enough canvas so you can work the pattern with plenty of room all around it. Follow the chart for each design and use the colors on the key.

When finished with each piece, cut out shape in the middle of the row next to the last finished row. Bind off around cut edges and through last worked rows.

Cut ribbon lengths approximately 10 inches long and stitch each end to the 2 parts of the design. One piece is inserted in the book, the other hangs out above the pages.

When working on the monogram project, refer to page 31 for alphabet letters.

Eyeglass case

A needlepoint eyeglass case is a perfect week-end project. A small print of red flowers on a bright blue background is used here. It's better to use regular needlepoint canvas than plastic as you'll want a soft, flexible item.

You'll need a piece of canvas at least 9 inches square to make the case, which is 3½ × 6½ inches.

Materials: Needlepoint canvas; 1–2–3 ply Persian-type yarn—2 skeins each of navy blue, red, and green, 1 skein yellow, 4 skeins light blue; needle; fabric for lining.

Directions

Mark center of canvas for fold line between front and back of case. Draw a rectangle around the canvas for the finished size.

Follow the chart and work row repeats in the Continental stitch for length of case. Continue by repeating the design until your needlepoint area measures 6½ × 7 inches. Block the needlepoint by steam pressing from the wrong side. Let dry thoroughly.

Trim canvas so you have ½ inch around finished work. Fold top edge to inside. Make a mitered cut through each corner and fold back all edges along stitches. With wrong sides together fold case at center line of canvas. Stitch together along bottom and then stitch side edges with a whipstitch. Make an extra stitch in the top corner hole.

Lining

Cut lining piece 7 × 7 inches. With right sides facing fold fabric in half lengthwise. Stitch across bottom and side with ½-inch seam allowance. Trim. Fold top edge out ½ inch and slip lining inside case. Canvas and lining are now right side out. Line up side seams and stitch lining to case along top edge.

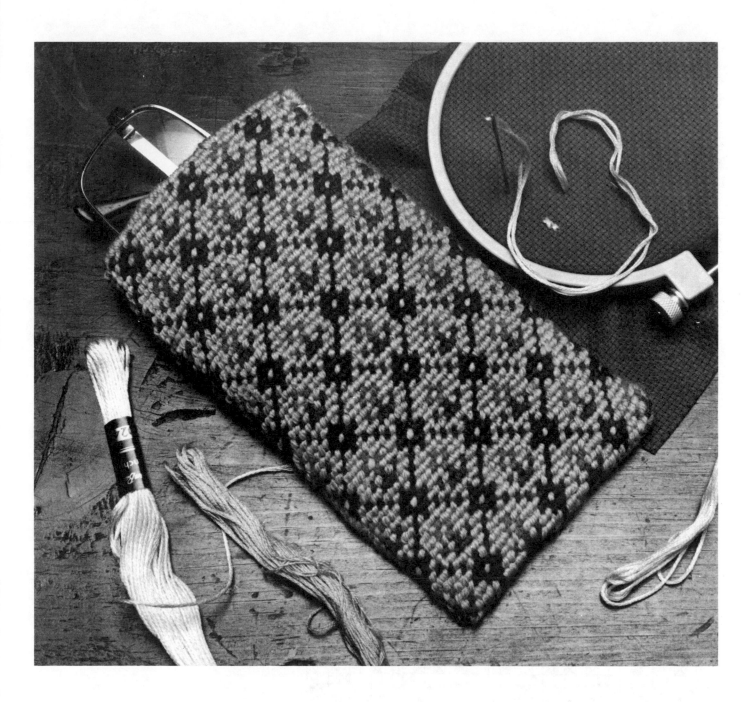

Eyeglass case

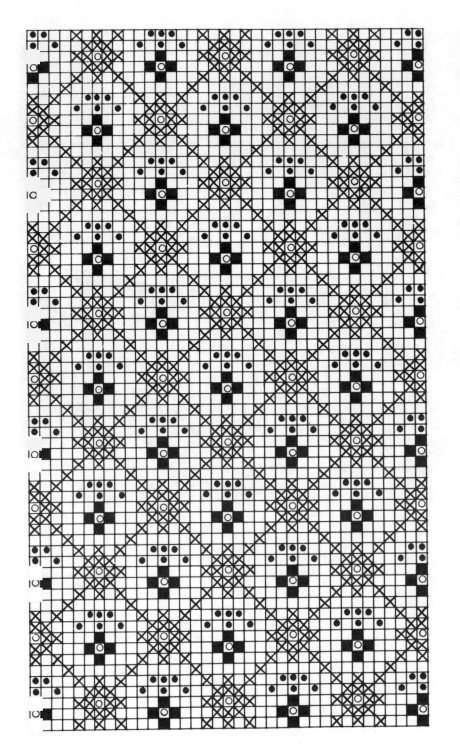

light blue

dark blue

yellow

green

red

38

Dainty change purse

Dainty change purse

Make this striking change purse from a small piece of plastic canvas, then line it with a soft fabric such as satin or printed cotton.

The black background with the bright pink flowers and green leaves will appeal to anyone on your gift list.

Materials: 10-count plastic canvas; 1–2–3 ply Persian-type yarn—1 skein each of pink and green, 2 skeins black; needle; small piece of lining fabric; snap for closure.

Directions

The purse is slightly under 6 inches wide and 4 inches high. Use a piece of canvas that is larger and follow the chart for color and placement of stitches.

When finished cut around the design according to the pattern. Repeat pattern for back piece and cut out shape when finished.

Lining

Place the cutout purse shape on the fabric and cut 2 pattern pieces. With right sides facing, stitch fabric together around edges but not across the top. Clip fabric around curves. Turn top edge to outside ¼ inch and press. Set aside.

Finish

With wrong sides facing, bind front and back of needlepoint canvas together with black yarn all around curved edges and bottom. Bind off around top edge of opening (do not stitch together).

Set lining piece into purse and stitch along top edge. If you make this a bright pink lining it will be a nice surprise when the purse is opened.

Attach a snap closure to either side of the top inside center.

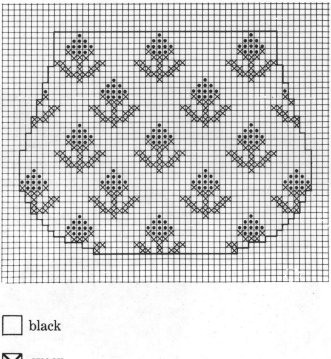

□ black

☒ green

◉ pink

I suppose teddy bears will be popular forever. This little juggling bear holding three hearts with a message is easy to make with plastic canvas. Then simply cut out the shape and use it as a tree ornament or propped in a basket of greens for a centerpiece. It will also make a delightful decoration on your front door to welcome holiday guests.

Materials: 10-count plastic canvas; 1–2–3 ply Persian-type yarn—1 skein each of brown and white, 2 skeins red; needle; felt for backing, and ribbon (optional).

Directions

You will need a full sheet of plastic canvas so you'll have plenty of room to work and cut out the design when finished.

Follow chart and work with the Continental stitch. When finished cut around outside shape and bind off all edges using the same color yarn as design.

Carefully cut out canvas area around inside of design. Use small snipping scissors to do this. Bind off edges with appropriate yarn colors.

Finish

If using this as an ornament you will want to finish the back with a felt piece. Place the finished design on felt and draw around the shape. Cut this out slightly smaller and glue or stitch to back of needlepoint. Add a small ribbon loop to top for hanging.

☐ white

⬤ brown

☒ red

■ black

Counted cross-stitch

The technique of cross-stitch is perhaps the most popular among needleworkers. This is because it is easy to do and the results are always perfect. Every stitch is exactly like the others, and the finished project is neat and crisp.

You don't need a printed design on fabric as with embroidery, or a painted design on canvas as with needlepoint. The design is charted on graph paper and each square represents an X stitch on fabric. No enlarging is necessary. You simply count the number of squares off on your chart and work them in a corresponding manner on an even-weave fabric such as Hardanger or Aida (available in needlework stores and some five and tens). Any checked fabric such as gingham is also excellent for cross-stitch; the size of the checks will determine how large your design will be. Since each stitch fills one square, large checked fabrics are not suitable.

For best results use a blunt-end embroidery needle, an embroidery hoop to keep work taut, and 6-strand embroidery floss from DMC or Coats and Clark.

Stitch all lines slanted in the same direction and then the other. All top threads should cross over in the same direction. Some projects will require all 6 strands; others look best with 2 or 3. Begin each project by separating the strands and putting together the numbers required. Use lengths of thread that feel comfortable to work with.

Framed fruit

Make a little cross-stitch fruit design, and finish with a colorful snap-together frame that can also be used as an embroidery hoop to do the work. A color chart is provided for the design.

The cross-stitch is approximately 3 × 4 inches and can fill a small space in the kitchen or dining area.

The strawberry design framed in red or green is a delightful handmade gift. Once you make one, you'll want to make another for yourself.

Materials: 12-count Aida cloth in ecru color; embroidery floss (see chart); embroidery needle; hoop.

Directions

Begin by separating the 6-strand floss. Use 3 strands for these projects. Locate the center or find a starting point of the design. Be sure to position it on your Aida so that you have plenty of room for framing.

Each stitch is coded to a color for correct placement. Sometimes I find it necessary to color in each square or line on the chart as it is worked. In this way I don't lose track of where I am. If you think you'll use the design again, pencil in the squares and erase when the project is finished.

With the Aida cloth held tautly in the embroidery hoop bring needle up from under side through one corner hole. Leave a tail about ½ inch long. Do not knot beginning or end threads. When finished, weave last inch or so under existing threads on wrong side. Continue to make slanted lines from corner to corner in one color area. Cross all lines in the opposite direction to make X stitches. Fill in all areas of one color before moving on to another color and section.

Finish

When completely stitched, place face down on ironing board and steam press on wrong side.

Trim cloth to fit frame. These frames, called Flexi-Hoops, come in eight different colors and sizes.

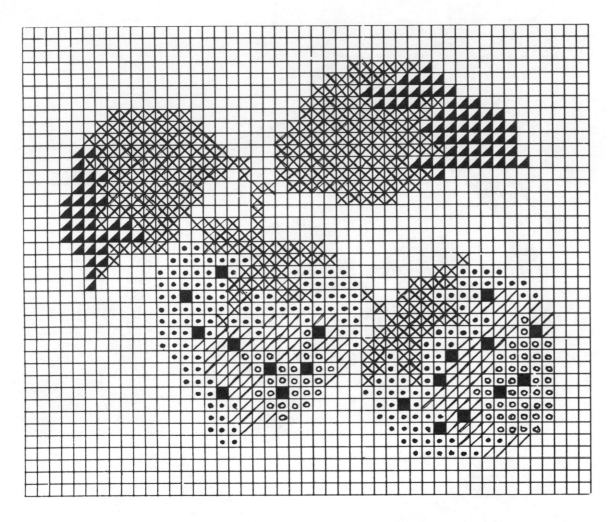

 deep red

 medium red

 pink

medium green

light green

black

Once you start cross-stitching you won't want to stop. It's easy to pick it up in odd moments and the results are so crisp and perfect. This design is worked in red and black. The letters and the X on the jacket are left white. A green row outlines the Noel sign.

Materials: 12-count white Aida cloth; red, black, and green embroidery floss; needle; hoop; red felt, 2½ × 5½ inches; red piping, 20 inches; ¼ inch satin ribbon, 4 inches long; polyfil stuffing.

Directions

Separate floss to work with 3 strands that are 12–15 inches long. With Aida in hoop, find starting point and follow the chart to fill in stitches. The color key indicates placement of colors. See directions on pages 43 and 44.

When design is finished, remove from hoop and iron on wrong side. With raw edges aligned, pin piping to front of cross-stitch piece. Stitch around. Pin red felt to front and stitch around all edges with a ¼-inch seam allowance, leaving the top edge open. Turn right side out.

Stuff ornament so it is slightly puffy. Fold a 4-inch piece of ribbon in half and insert ends into top opening. Stitch closed and hang.

black ☒

red ■

green ▣

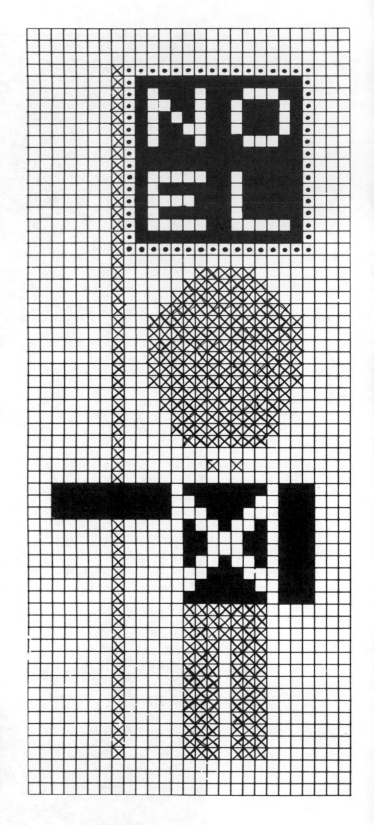

Poinsettia tray

You can make a design to fit inside any size tray and have a glass piece cut to fit over it. The finished piece here is 12 × 17½ inches. This is a good size for a place mat as well. The cross-stitched poinsettia makes a nice bright design for a Christmas tray and the border design can be used on matching napkins if desired.

Cross-stitch can be deceiving: Sometimes a simple project like this one looks quicker than it is. I suggest you make one place mat well before Christmas. This will help you estimate how many you can actually make in the time you have available. The tray is a very special handmade gift and will surely be treasured for years by the recipients.

Materials: 12-count white Aida cloth; 3 skeins of red and 1 skein of green embroidery floss; needle; hoop; tray; glass.

Directions

The color key will tell you where to place the stitches. Use a piece of Aida larger than the tray inset in order to hem all around when finished.

Fold the fabric in half in one direction and in half again in the other to find the center of cloth.

Center design on fabric and adjust border to fit your tray. The design can also be used as is for a holiday place mat.

When finished, press from wrong side and turn edges under all around. Press and stitch along fold line to hold hem in place. Put in tray with glass on top to protect the cloth.

If you're making a place mat, cut a piece of red or green fabric the same size as unfinished cloth. Turn all edges to inside and stitch around close to the fold line. Press.

Linen napkins are excellent for even-weave counted cross-stitch. Make a white border on red napkins for a nice contrast.

■ green   ☒ red

Every baby is a sweet little angel and deserves a special dress-up bib for the holidays. This "little angel" design can be worked up in no time and looks good in any color combination. You can make your own bib from Aida cloth with the pattern provided. Or, you can purchase one ready to stitch. Needlework and notions stores often carry this item.

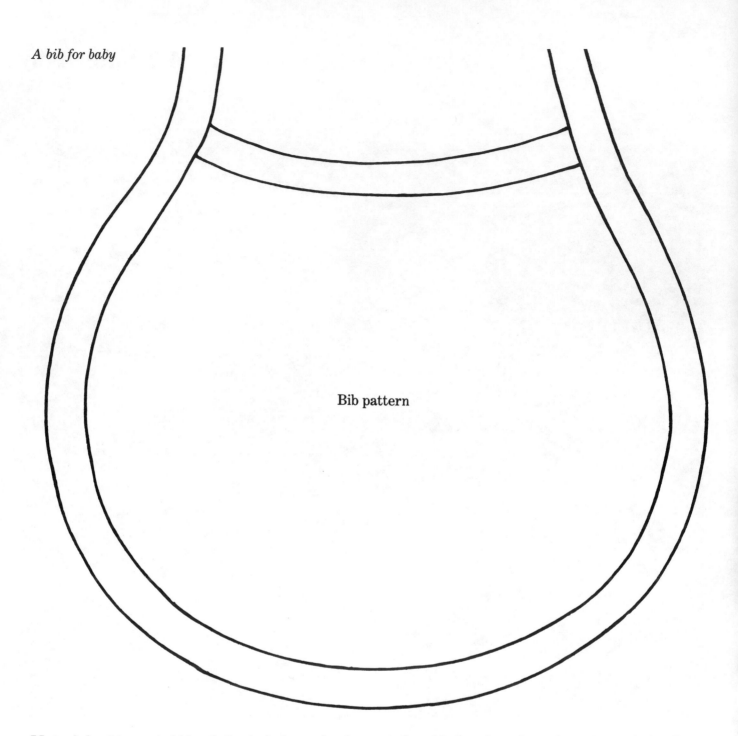

Bib pattern

Materials: 14-count Aida cloth; 1 skein each of embroidery floss (see color key); needle; hoop; ¼-inch bias binding in color of your choice; small piece of matching cotton fabric same size as bib.

Directions

It is easiest to work the cross-stitch design before cutting out the bib pattern. In this way you will have enough fabric around the design to fit comfortably in the embroidery hoop.

Follow the charted design and refer to color key for placement of stitches. Separate floss and use 3 strands for this project. Begin from the underside and do not make a knot. Leave a 1-inch tail and bring thread up through one hole. Cross to diagonal hole and continue to make slanted stitches in one direction. Finish stitches with all threads going in the same direction. (See general directions on page 43.)

Be sure to count accurately for placement of words. When finished, press from wrong side.

Trace the pattern for bib and place it on top of cross-stitch. Center the design and pin pattern to it. Pin to cotton fabric and cut out bib shape.

Stitch front and back together with hem facing, leaving enough on either side of neck for tying.

	pink		black
	light blue		yellow
	light green		flesh

Place mats and napkins

Make one, two, or a set of four place mats with easy to sew cross-stitch borders and country hearts. The grid fabric is from the International Printworks (see the mail-order source list, page 160) and is 51-inch-wide cotton. I used the berry color with white design for this project. The finished place mat is 12 × 16 inches. An ample size for the napkins is 9 × 12 inches.

Materials: ½ yard of fabric for 4 place mats; ½ yard for 4 napkins; 2 skeins white embroidery floss; needle; hoop.

Directions

Cut a rectangle 12½ × 16½ inches. Turn edges under ¼ inch all around and press. Turn again ¼ inch and stitch to make finished place mat.

Separate 6-strand floss and work stitches with 4 strands. Refer to counted cross-stitch chart and stitch outside border along 4th row in from edge. Next count up 13 rows from stitched border and work inside border on the 14th row. Finish with hearts in each corner.

Napkins

Hem edges of napkin squares as with place mat. Cross-stitch border around 3rd row in from finished edge. Refer to chart for placement of one heart in the corner. Alternate chart of row of tulips works on the diagonal and can be used for both napkins and place mats.

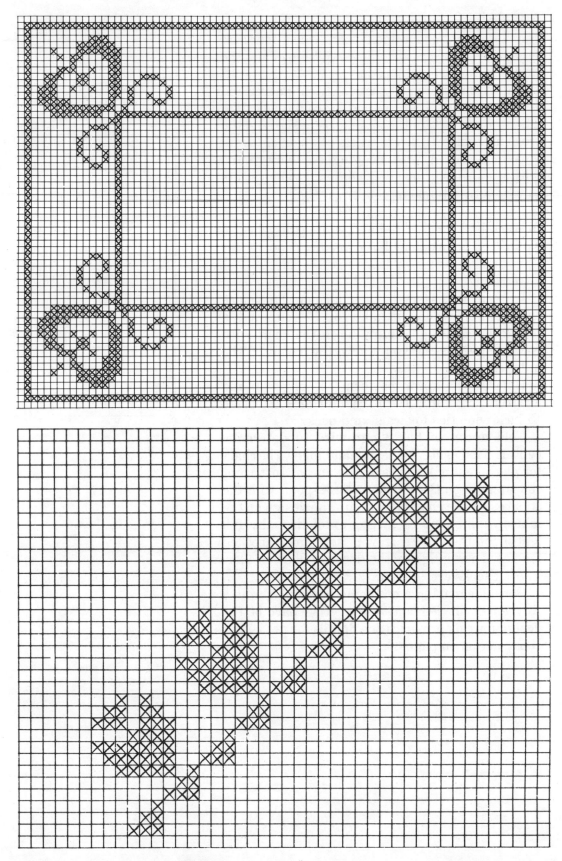

Flowering apron

When cross-stitch is done in one color it has a completely different look than when multicolored. This fabric is a red and white grid and the design is worked in all red.

The grid fabric makes cross-stitch quicker and easier than any other method for counted design. The squares dictate the size of the design and the work is easier to keep track of than on even-weave fabric. A grid or gingham background with a solid color design is contemporary yet fits in with a traditional or country feeling.

Materials: 1 yard of red and white grid fabric; 5 skeins red embroidery floss; needle; hoop.

Directions

It is not necessary to have a color chart since the design is done in all red. If you want a multicolored design simply fill in the chart with colored pencils so you know the color of the stitches.

Enlarge the apron pattern (see page 14) and cut from the fabric. Hem around edges and make ½-inch-wide ties for waist and neck.

Fold apron in half lengthwise to determine center. Find center of design and follow the chart for placement of stitches on the apron. Just count the squares on the fabric to correspond with the squares on the charted design. The design on the fabric will be quite large, extending the full length of the front. If you use small checked fabric such as gingham the design will be smaller. These checks are ¼ inch.

Consider making a matching pot holder from a tiny check in red and white. Use part of the design for this project. (See details for pot holder construction on page 60.)

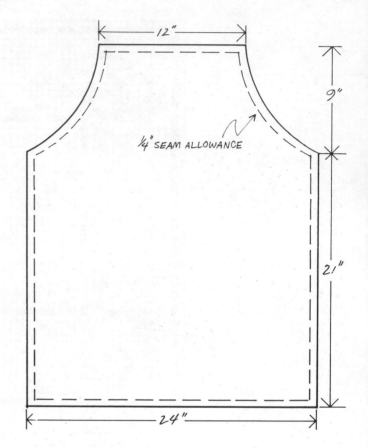

Flowering apron

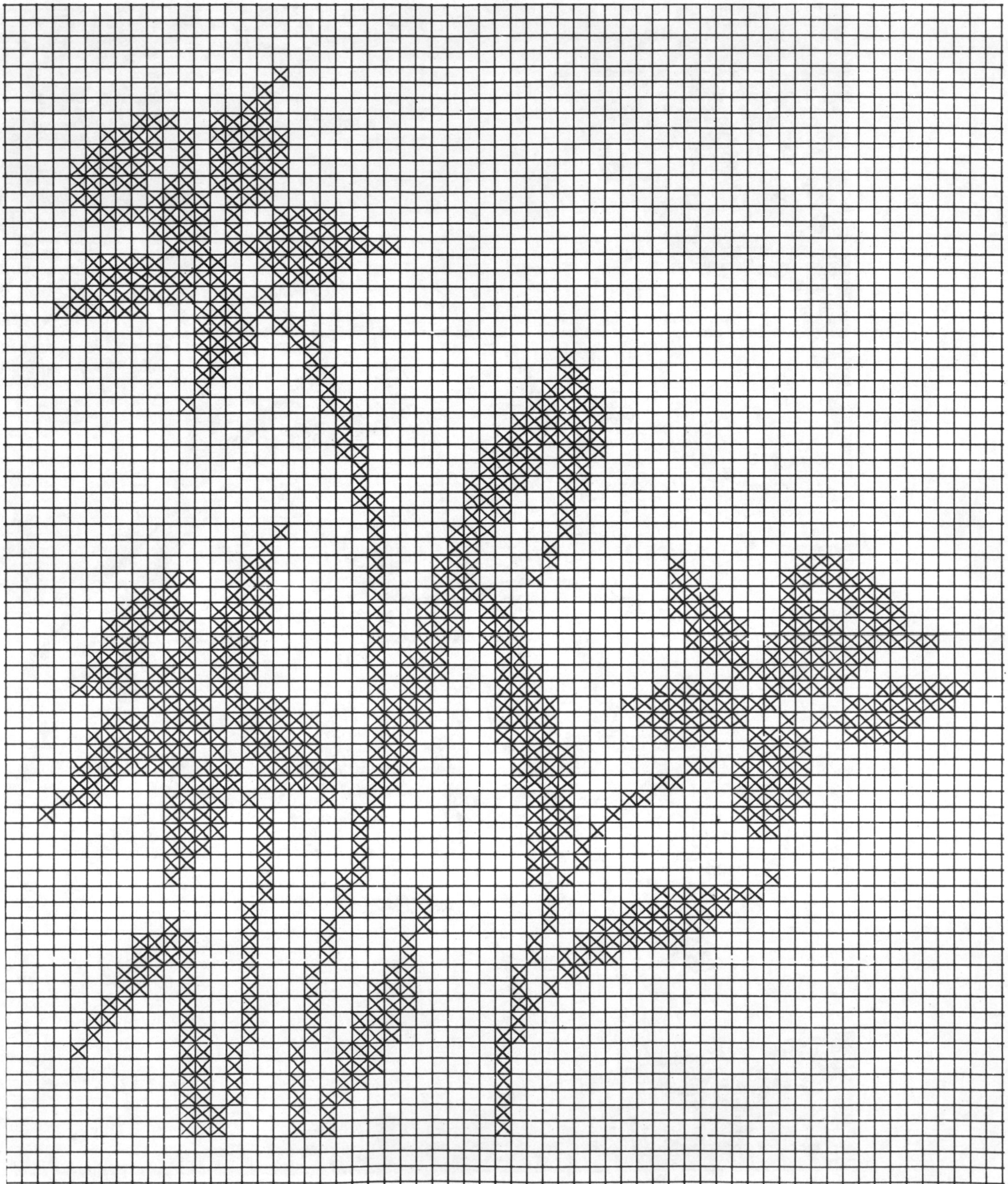

Kitchen set

A toaster cover and pot holder are useful gifts that can be made special with lovely fabric and cross-stitch designs. Made in one color on grid fabric the design is versatile enough to be used on place mats, curtains, and an apron as well. The pot holder is a quick and easy last-minute gift.

You can use any checked fabric such as gingham; the design will be larger or smaller depending on the size of the checks. This fabric is from the International Printworks (see the mail-order source list, page 160) and comes in a variety of designer colors with white ruled lines. The squares are ¼ inch.

Materials for toaster cover: ¼ yard of grid fabric; 2 skeins white embroidery floss; needle; hoop; ¼-inch cording; small piece of contrasting fabric for trim.

Directions

Measure all sides of your toaster, including front, top, and sides. Leaving ½ inch extra all around, cut 2 pieces of fabric for the front and back.

With ½-inch seam allowance cut a long piece to fit up one end, across the top, and down the other end. You may prefer ¼-inch or ⅜-inch seam allowance but I always give myself a full ½ inch. Sometimes it depends on the fabric.

Cut 2 pieces of cording the same length as the long strip of fabric. Cover each piece of cording with a contrasting or matching grid fabric.

Pin the cording to the right side of fabric with raw edges aligned. Using a zipper foot, stitch over the first stitching, beginning and ending 1 inch from the ends. Open the fabric-covered cording and cut the cord ends. Turn end of fabric under ½ inch and restitch.

Cross-stitch

Using all 6 strands of floss, follow the diagram to make counted cross-stitch design on the front of the toaster cover. Each square represents one square on the grid fabric. Count the squares on the design and fabric to determine where to start. Remember to leave enough fabric around the design to sew all pattern pieces together.

For cross-stitch directions, see page 43.

Finish

With right sides facing, stitch front piece of fabric to one edge of long strip. Repeat for back piece of toaster cover. Turn right side out. Turn bottom edge under ¼ inch and press. Turn under another ¼ inch and stitch for finished hem.

Materials for pot holder: ¼ yard of grid fabric (or scraps from toaster cover); 6¼ × 6¼–inch piece of fabric in contrasting color; 1 skein embroidery floss; embroidery hoop; needle; polyfil or quilt batting.

Directions

The finished pot holder is 8 × 8 inches and has 3 layers of batting for thickness. This is a generous size and well padded. I used 2 colors of the same grid fabric. The border is lavender and the center square is blue.

Before cutting fabric pieces, work cross-stitch design. In this way you have enough fabric to fit in the embroidery hoop. Follow the stitch placement chart and see pages 43 and 44 for cross-stitch directions. Work design on contrasting 6¼ × 6¼–inch fabric.

Cut 2 pieces of fabric 8¼ × 8¼ inches. Cut filler piece 8 × 8 inches. Cut small piece of fabric 1½ × 4 inches for hanging loop. Ribbon or a plastic curtain ring can be used for this, but the matching fabric looks pretty.

Turn edges of 8¼ square under ¼ inch and press. Pin together with batting between. Turn edges of cross-stitch piece under ¼ inch all around and pin to center of pot holder (see photo for placement). You will have a square of one color surrounded by a border of the background color.

Fold 1½ × 4–inch fabric piece in half lengthwise and press with wrong sides facing. Turn long raw edges inside ¼ inch and press. Stitch along edge. Fold in half to create a 2-inch loop and insert between pot holder layers at one corner. Pin to hold.

Stitch around outside edge of pot holder, catching loop in one corner. Stitch around outside edge of center square. Stitch around cross-stitch design. This will create a quilted effect.

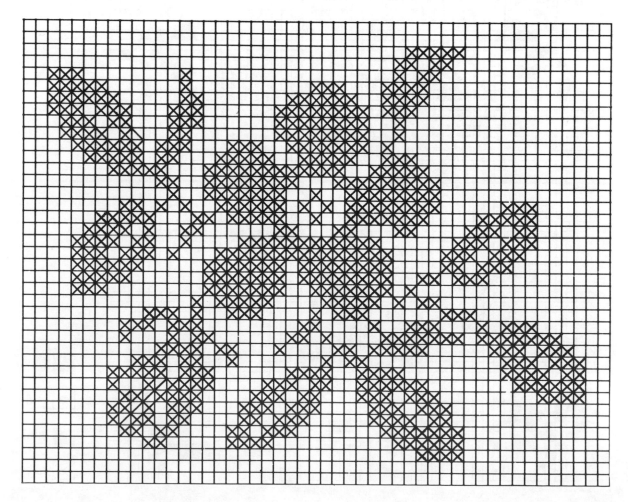

Cross-stitch sachet

A small, delicate flower with corner borders is made to look like a painted tile design. Make several to give with delicate lingerie or to tuck in a stocking. If you add a ribbon loop you can use this as a tree ornament for Christmas and then tuck it away for sweet-smelling drawers after the holidays.

Materials: 12-count Aida cloth; ½ yard of lace; 5 × 5–inch blue cotton piece for backing; ½ × 20–inch blue strip of cotton for piping; embroidery floss—1 skein each of light green, dark green, pink, red, yellow, bright blue; embroidery hoop; needle; cotton filling; potpourri; ribbon (optional).

Directions

Work on Aida before cutting out square. Separate 6-strand floss and use 3 strands to cross stitch on the fabric following the chart and color key. (See general directions on page 43 for cross-stitch.)

With design centered, cut a 5-inch square from the Aida. Fold blue strip of fabric in half lengthwise and press. Stitch ends to create a loop. Pin to front of design so edges align. Stitch around all edges.

Next stitch edges of lace together to make a loop. Pin to top of design with piping between. Machine baste.

With right sides facing, sew blue square on top, leaving 2 inches in center of one edge open. Trim corners, turn, and fill with cotton and potpourri. Add ribbon for hanging if desired.

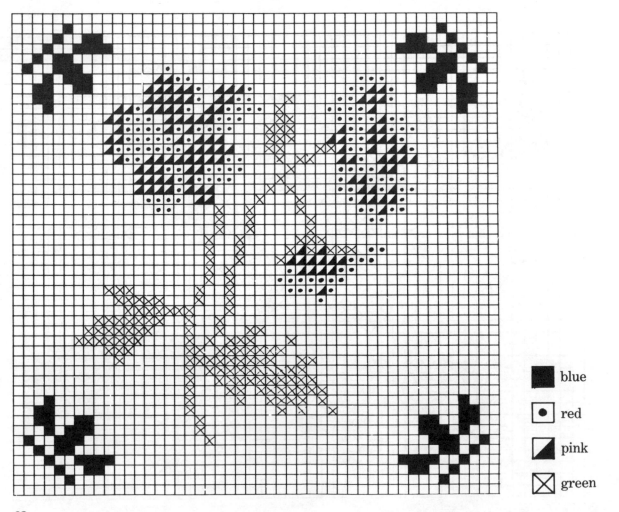

■	blue
⊡	red
◩	pink
⊠	green

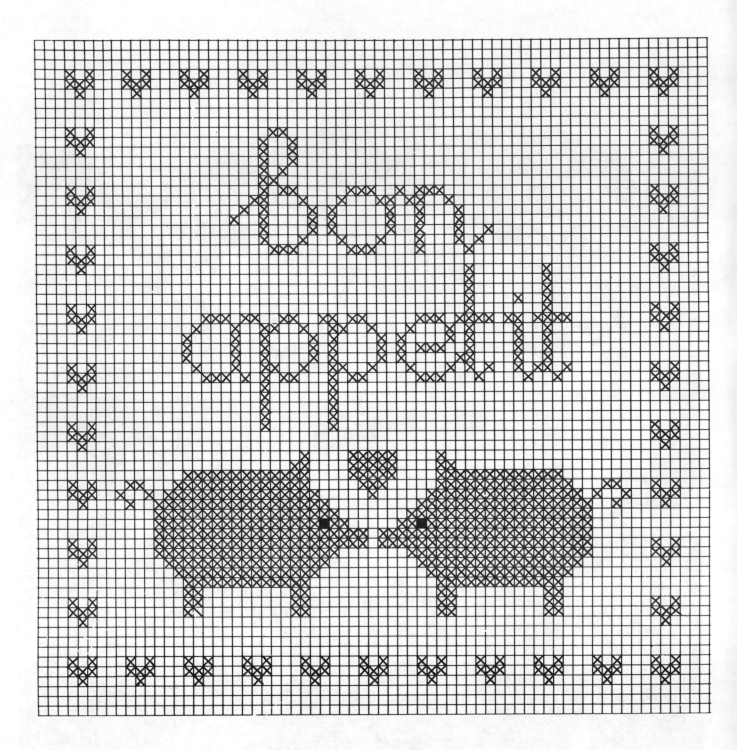

Bon appetit plaque

Our pigs in love on pink gingham is a cross-stitch sign to enhance any kitchen. The smallest check gingham is used with pink floss. Since the gingham comes in all colors, select the one that matches your kitchen or that of the friend who will receive this darling gift.

Materials: ¼ yard of pink gingham; 2 skeins pink embroidery floss; picture frame; needle; hoop.

Directions

Use all 6 embroidery strands and work the design according to chart. Simply count the stitches to correspond to the checks on the graph and fabric for placement. Do the center first and the border last to be sure of perfect centering.

Cut fabric to ½ inch of border all around. Turn under and press from wrong side. Place fabric right side up on cardboard backing (comes with frame) and place glass and frame over all.

Wood appliqué

Give your home a special touch with one of these country accents made with balsa wood and Rit dye. It's easy and fun to create authentic-looking reproductions of country accessories like the welcome sign that looks like one you'd find in the entrance to an early New England home. Or, serve guests on a tray decorated with a basketful of fruit dyed in bright country colors. An old-fashioned checkerboard doesn't have to be an antique to lend charm to your room. Create your own with a few simple directions.

Because the balsa is easy to cut and dye you can make illustrations as with fabric, but you get a layered, three-dimensional effect. You can also use this technique to make pictures for a child's room, trivets, Christmas ornaments, and gift tags.

General directions

Balsa wood comes in 4 × 36–inch strips and all thicknesses. These projects are made from $1/16$-inch–thick balsa.

Rit liquid dye colors are exquisite and the balsa comes out as brilliant or as subtle as you want. Just dip the balsa strips in the hot solution as you would with fabric. Let dry.

Tip: A long plastic pan used for wallpaper hanging is perfect for dying balsa strips. It's an inexpensive, throwaway item found in most home-center or wallpaper stores.

Trace pattern pieces and transfer to balsa pieces in the following way:
1. Tape pattern to dyed piece of balsa.
2. With ballpoint pen retrace around outline of design using slight pressure. The balsa wood is soft and will have the impression of the design outline where traced.
3. Place balsa on a cutting surface and cut out each design element with an X-Acto knife. Continue to cut each piece from the color that corresponds to the pattern piece.

If you're making ornaments or gift tags, consider using cookie cutters for patterns. For example, place a Christmas tree cookie cutter on bright-green-dyed balsa and draw around the shape. Cut it out. Punch a hole in the top with a paper punch and tie with yarn or ribbon. You have a wonderful country-style tree ornament. Since you'll dye a whole strip of balsa at once, you can get quite a few ornaments from it.

This early-American sign is perfect for welcoming guests. Since it isn't weatherproof it can hang in a hall or entranceway or on an inside door.

You'll need a jigsaw or coping saw to cut the wood shape, which is made from 1-inch pine. You can also take the pattern to a lumberyard or framer to be cut. The finished size is 9½ inches at the center and 16 inches long.

Materials: Scrap piece of 1 × 10–inch pine; tracing paper; 4 × 36–inch strip of balsa wood for each color; acrylic paint (white and cream); 1-inch paintbrush; Rit powder or liquid dyes—purple, green, yellow, red, brown; India ink; X-Acto knife, #11 blade; fine-point marker; glue.

Directions

Enlarge pattern and transfer to wood. Cut out with a jigsaw or coping saw. Sand rough edges. Paint all surfaces with cream color acrylic paint.

Mix dye according to directions on package or bottle and dye strips of balsa. Paint one 6-inch-long piece white for the church and fence.

Trace "Welcome" on tracing paper and transfer to front of plaque (see page 14). Using India ink, fill in sign lettering. Let dry. Follow general directions for cutting pattern pieces (page 66).

Pattern sequence

Make each house complete before gluing.

1. Cut out all house, school, and church shapes (front piece).
2. Cut same shapes again from window colors (back piece).
3. Cut out window shapes from the front pieces.
4. Glue front to back pieces.
5. Cut out roof and glue on top of front piece. Glue details like clock on schoolhouse to front pieces.
6. Draw details such as siding on the houses with a fine-point marker.
7. Cut out all tree shapes.
8. Use a marker to make lines every $\frac{1}{4}$ inch on a $\frac{5}{8}$-inch-high strip for fence.
9. Place a strip of masking tape along bottom edge to create a straight line. Place pieces in position.
10. Glue center building to the plaque and work outward to either end. Cut fence pieces to fit as you go along.

Finish

Drill hole in center top from back so it doesn't go all the way through to the front. Hang on a small nail.

black

ivory

Each square equals 1″.

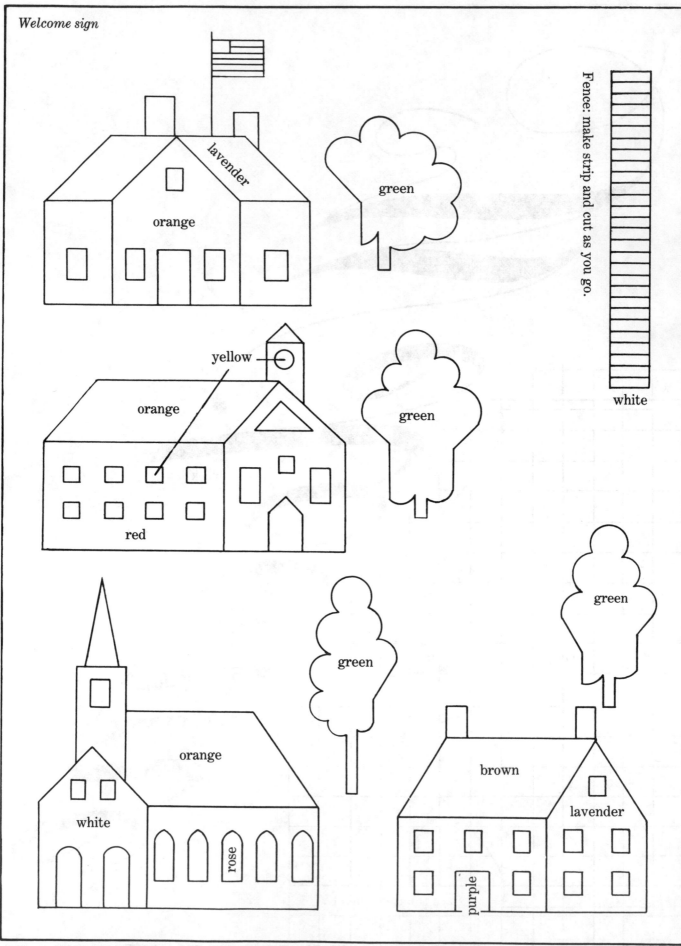

Fence: make strip and cut as you go.

white

lavender

orange

green

yellow

orange

red

green

green

green

orange

white

rose

brown

lavender

purple

This reproduction of an old salt holder is a good item for a pretty floral design. There are many such items—cannisters, recipe boxes, breadboxes, among others—that can be enhanced with this appliqué technique.

Materials: Wood container; 3 strips balsa wood; liquid dye—pink, yellow, green; 1-inch paintbrush; tracing paper; craft knife; glue; varnish and raw umber (optional).

Directions

Remember that you can get many different shades of a color from one package of dye. With just two or three colors you can create a much wider variety of lights and darks. The pink and red flowers are a result of leaving one strip of balsa in the dye a little longer than the other.

See general directions on page 66 for cutting and positioning dyed balsa pieces. Follow pattern and color keys. When dying a three-dimensional object you can brush the dye on the item rather than submerge it.

To antique

Coat the box with varnish and let dry overnight. Reapply varnish.

Brush acrylic raw umber across each side and wipe away the excess; this leaves subtle antiquing streaks. Let dry and revarnish.

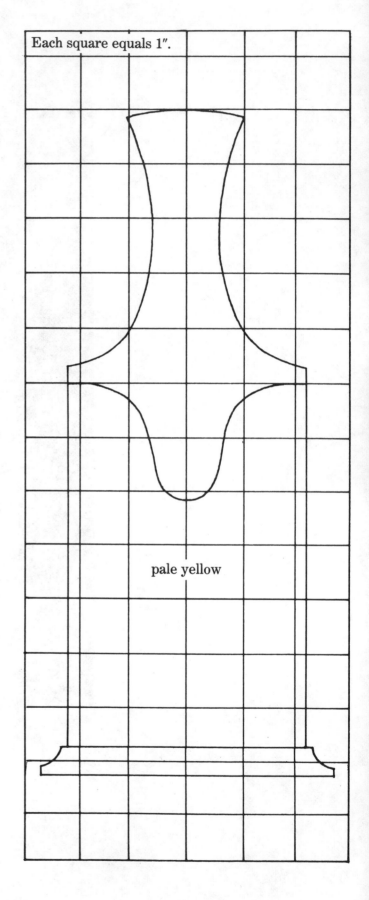

Each square equals 1″.

pale yellow

73

Folk sign

This is another version of a country welcome sign. The cutout illustration pieces are glued to a pine plaque.

Materials: 1-inch pine, 11 × 16 inches; 1 strip each of balsa wood dyed green, purple, orange, and red; tracing paper; cream color acrylic paint; 1-inch paintbrush; glue.

Directions

Paint front of plaque. See general directions on page 66 for dying balsa, tracing, and transferring letters to balsa wood.

Center sign and glue letters in place. Follow the pattern for color placement.

Finish

With purple balsa cut 1-inch-wide strips to make a border and edge the plaque. Glue strips in place. Let dry thoroughly before hanging.

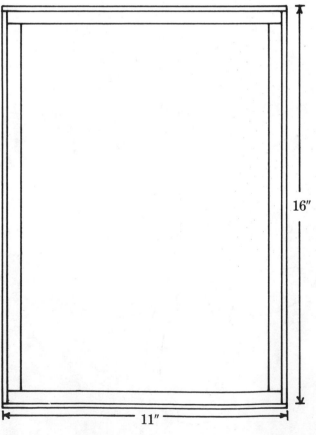

16″

11″

orange

purple

WELCOME

red

blue

pink

green

brown

green

red

orange

red

pink

brown

lavender

purple

red

purple

Quilt-pattern trivet

Use any geometric quilt pattern to create a patchwork trivet. The finished size is 8 × 8 inches and all pieces fit together like a puzzle.

Materials: 1-inch pine plaque, 8 × 8 inches; 4 strips of ¹⁄₁₆-inch balsa wood; 1 strip of ⅛-inch balsa wood; tracing paper; green, red, yellow, and pink dye; craft knife; glue.

Directions

See general directions on page 66. Dye the ⅛-inch strip green and set aside to edge plaque. Cut all pieces and glue in position on plaque. Glue edging all around.

yellow

olive green

burnt orange

pink

Basketful of fruit

You can create a sensational tray from a very ordinary one. The basket and pieces of fruit are all cut out and arranged to sit on a table. The finished project is 12 × 17½ inches.

Materials: Tray; glass piece cut to fit inside dimensions; tracing paper; 1 strip of ⅛-inch balsa wood; 8 strips of ¹⁄₁₆-inch balsa wood; 1 package each of purple, red, orange, green, brown, ecru, blue, and yellow dye; black marker; glue.

Directions

Refer to general directions on page 66 for transferring designs and cutting out pattern pieces from dyed balsa. You will note that some of the fruit pieces overlap the basket. These areas will be ⅛ inch in thickness, raising them slightly. The border is dyed blue and made from the ⅛-inch-thick balsa piece. This raises the level of the design evenly all around so a glass piece can be set over the design.

The background is made from the one piece of balsa that is left natural. The bottom portion of the tray, the table, is ecru. Refer to the color key when gluing pieces in position.

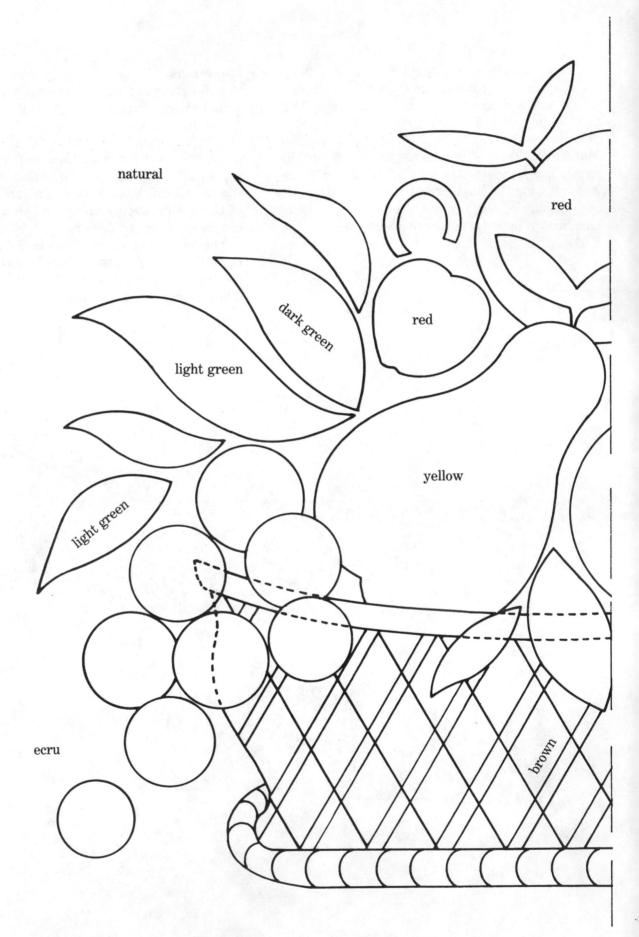

natural

red

dark green

red

light green

yellow

light green

ecru

brown

p. 67

p. 154

p. 90

p. 110

p. 62

p. 49

p. 113

WELCOME

p. 74

D·M

p. 29

p. 152

p. 118

p. 124

p. 134

p. 147

p. 84

p. 44

p. 54

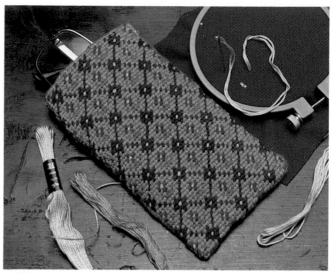

p. 36

p. 144

p. 64

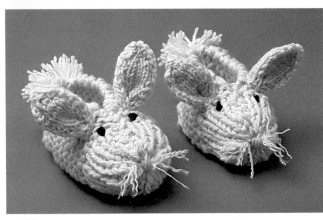

p. 132

p. 127

p. 51

p. 157

p. 41

p. 34

p. 32

p. 23

p. 39

p. 152

p. 20

p. 78

p. 26

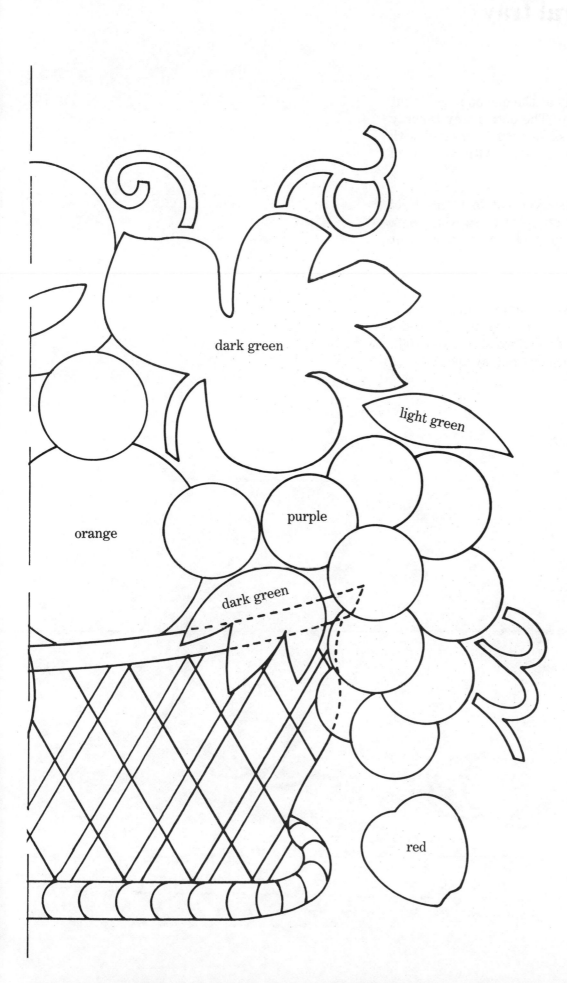

dark green

light green

orange

purple

dark green

red

Delicate floral tray

This is the same tray as the one on page 79 but with a different design. The entire tray is spray painted blue. A vine of flowers is created with green and pink balsa covered with a piece of glass.

Materials: Tray; glass piece cut to fit inside of tray; tracing paper; 2 strips of balsa wood; pink and green dye; blue enamel spray paint; craft knife; glue.

Directions

Spray entire tray with enamel paint. Let dry. Follow the pattern and color key and cut pieces from the dyed strips of balsa wood (see page 66).

Glue all pieces in place on the tray and set glass over all.

rose

kelly green

yellow

Checkerboard

You might almost think this is a real old game board. In fact, it's made from dyed balsa wood glued to a wooden plaque. Use these colors for a country look or create your own color scheme.

Materials: 1-inch pine plaque, 12 × 20 inches; 3 strips of 1/16-inch balsa wood; 1 strip of 1/8-inch balsa wood; tracing paper; dye—red, green, yellow, and purple; craft knife; glue.

Directions
See general directions on page 66 for dying, transferring, and cutting designs. Dye the 1/8-inch balsa purple.

Follow placement diagram for gluing squares in place. Glue green pieces at either end and wedge purple cross pieces in at each end of checkerboard. Glue purple 1/8-inch pieces around edge of plaque to make a border. The cross pieces and border are now at the same height. This creates a box at either end for holding checkers.

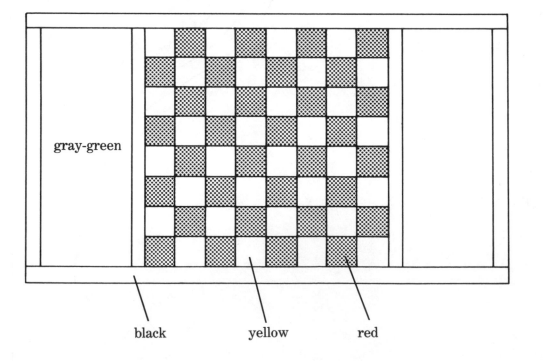

gray-green

black   yellow   red

Art deco mirror

Create a little interest with a flower-rimmed mirror. You can have any size mirror cut at your local glass shop. Glue a cardboard backing to it and trim with a design to finish the edges.

Materials: Round mirror (use a plate to create desired pattern size); 2 strips of balsa wood; green and red dye; cardboard; craft knife; glue; tracing paper.

Directions

Follow general directions on page 66. When dying red strip for flower petals, cut in 2 pieces and vary the length of soaking time to create different shades of the same color.

Cut a piece of cardboard the same size as the mirror and glue to back. Cut border in sections. Piece together as you glue them around the mirror's edge.

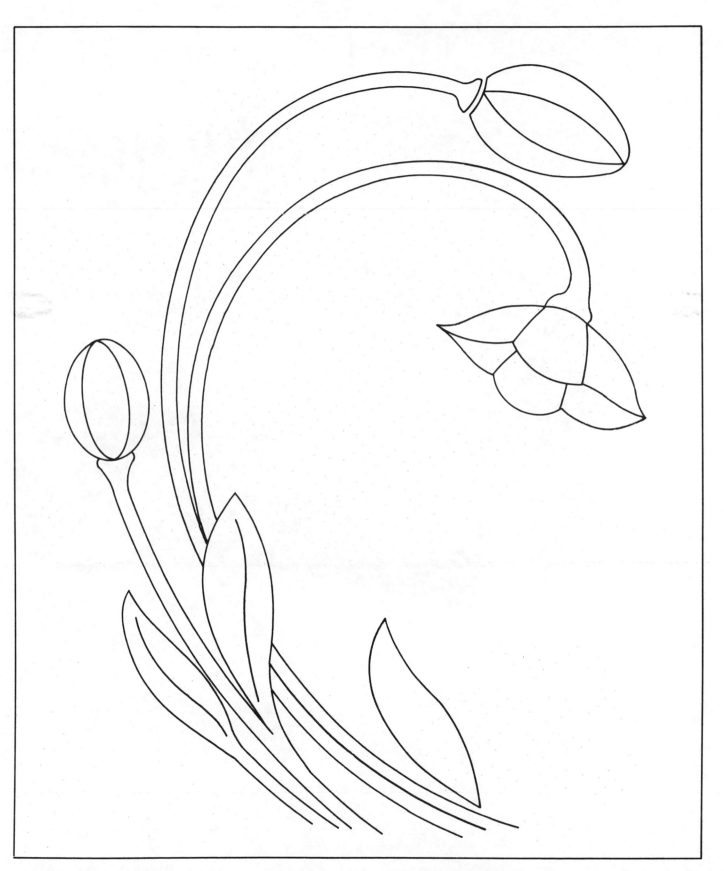

Stenciling

Stenciling is a process of applying designs to a surface. The stenciler places a cutout pattern on an object such as a piece of furniture, a wall, or a small box and fills in the cutout areas with paint. In this way an exact and perfect design can be repeated as many times as desired to produce an ornamental effect.

This is a wonderful and inexpensive way to add color and interest to small gift items. All the projects here use acrylic paint, which is equally good on a wooden surface and on fabric.

There are precut stencils sold as kits but each project presented here has an original design for you to trace and cut out. You can then use these stencils on a variety of projects of different sizes.

All stencil materials are available in art stores. To cut a stencil design you will need stencil paper. This is a wax-coated, slightly stiff paper that prevents the design from slipping while you work with it on a surface. It is excellent for large projects such as walls. Oak tag, Mylar, and acetate can also be used. Oak tag, manila folders, and acetate sleeves such as those used in photo albums are fairly inexpensive.

For cutting you will need an X-Acto craft knife with a #11 blade and a cutting surface.

Stencil brushes come in various sizes; for the following projects you will need two or three small ones. (See general directions for stencil supplies on page 16.)

The paint is applied to the cutout areas by tapping the brush up and down onto the surface. When the stencil sheet is removed, the design is accurately positioned with clean, sharp, well-defined edges.

Preparing the stencils takes more time than the actual crafting, so you might consider working on several projects at once. This way, once a stencil design is cut you can use it over and over, varying the placement and arrangement so each appears differently.

What-not boxes

Wooden or tin boxes come in all shapes and sizes, some with hinged tops, some with removable tops. You might even find jewelry boxes with drawers or metal recipe file boxes with hinges. If your local craft store doesn't carry them, see page 160 for a mail-order source.

Stenciling a design on a small box is an easy way to create a special gift. Choose colors that complement the room it may go in. Or, you might like to make the Christmas designs in bright red and green on white for the holidays. Then fill the box with candies or put some favorite recipes inside.

90

Materials: A variety of boxes; tracing paper; stencil paper; various colors of acrylic paint; 1-inch paintbrush (sponge brushes are inexpensive and available in all hardware stores); X-Acto knife; small stencil brush; Krylon clear spray varnish (optional); small piece of felt for bottom; paper, fabric, or paint for lining.

Directions

Paint the box inside and out. Let dry. Trace the design and transfer (see page 14) each color element to separate pieces of stencil paper. For example, the leaves for the flowers are one stencil and the petals create another stencil.

Tape the stencil paper design to a cutting board or several layers of newspaper on a hard surface. Cut out each element with the X-Acto knife. Position one of the designs on the box and tape at the corners to hold.

Applying paint

Squirt a small amount of paint onto a flat dish. Tap the stencil brush on the paint and then on newspaper a few times to remove excess paint. There should be a very small amount of paint on your brush.

Hold the stencil paper down with one hand and tap the brush up and down on the cutout area. The paint should go on lightly; it is best to apply it with many tapping motions rather than saturate the surface. When the first color is dry, place the original tracing over the box as a guide to position the next design element.

Place the second stencil over the tracing. Remove the tracing paper and tape the stencil down. Repeat the painting process.

Finishing

When the paint is dry, protect the surface with 3 or 4 coats of spray varnish. The inside can be left as is or you can add a paper or fabric lining. Complete directions can be found on page 94.

Cut a small piece of felt (five-and-tens always have felt squares at Christmas time) and glue to the bottom. If you're lining the box with paper you can finish the bottom with the paper rather than felt. Spray varnish over the paper to protect it.

Desk boxes

There are many different kinds of boxes that can be decorated for a variety of uses. For the man in your life you might decorate a wooden box with an American eagle or sailboat. This time I've used a reproduction Shaker box. It comes in different sizes and is excellent for many crafting projects. For a mail-order source, see page 160.

Materials: Wooden box (6- and 8-inch sizes used here); cream-colored latex or acrylic paint; 1-inch paintbrush; acrylic raw umber; clear spray varnish; black waterproof marker or India ink; tracing paper; glue and paper or fabric for lining (optional).

Directions

Give the box two coats of paint, allowing the first coat to dry thoroughly before repainting. You can paint the inside with the same color or a contrasting color. Or, plan to line the inside with paper or fabric (directions at end of project).

Trace the design and transfer to the box in the following way: Tape tracing so that the design is centered face down on the box. Next rub over the back of the design with a pencil. Remove tracing and go over the faint pencil line on the box.

Outline the design with black marker. Fill in the entire design with marker or India ink and let dry.

Spray 6 to 10 coats of varnish on all exposed areas. Let dry between coats (dries in minutes).

Antiquing

When the box is dry, antique with raw umber in the following way:

1. Squirt a small amount of umber on a paper plate or several layers of newspaper.
2. Use a slightly dampened clean brush and streak a small amount across the top area of the box.
3. With a wadded piece of paper toweling, wipe away the excess, leaving streaks of color here and there. It should be a subtle effect. Repeat on the sides and bottom half of the box. Let dry.
4. Apply one more coat of varnish to seal antiquing. Let dry thoroughly.

Lining

The easiest way to line the box is with a self-adhesive paper like ConTac, available in a variety of patterns and colors and found in five and ten and housewares stores. Other ways to have a pretty interior are to use wallpaper or wrapping paper.

Measure inside walls of top and bottom and cut paper strips slightly longer and deeper than measurement.

Use white glue to attach side pieces first. The excess can be trimmed with a razor blade once finished. Next cut and glue inside bottom pieces in position. Place the box on paper and draw around the bottom. Cut this piece and glue to the underside of box.

Let the paper dry for a half hour. Protect all paper with a coating of spray varnish. Let dry before using.

Padded lining

This is a very elegant way to finish the inside of your box. You will need a small amount of fabric. This can be a printed or solid cotton, velvet, satin, corduroy, etc. A small amount of quilt batting or polyfil, shirt cardboard, and glue are also needed.

First measure the inside walls and bottom area in top and bottom portions of the box. Next cut pieces of shirt cardboard slightly smaller than the measurements. Each piece will fit loosely when inserted. This allows room for the fabric covering.

Cut pieces of batting and attach to each cardboard piece with a drop of glue here and there. Cut pieces of fabric slightly larger than cardboard all around.

Spread small amounts of glue around back edges of each cardboard piece. With batting side down place on the back of corresponding fabric. Wrap fabric edges over cardboard to attach.

Spread small amount of glue on back of each fabric-covered cardboard piece. Place side pieces into the box first. Place bottom piece in position and press down. Finish underside of bottom with a piece of fabric or paper.

Note: To line box with felt, no cardboard is necessary. Cut felt pieces exactly to box measurement. Spread glue directly inside box area to be covered. Set felt pieces in place. Trim excess from top edges if necessary with a small snipping scissors.

It's simple to make luggage tags from fake leather. It cuts like butter and is easier to find than the real thing. Once you make the pattern you can cut out several for all pieces of luggage. Add a stenciled initial and you have identifiable luggage at a glance.

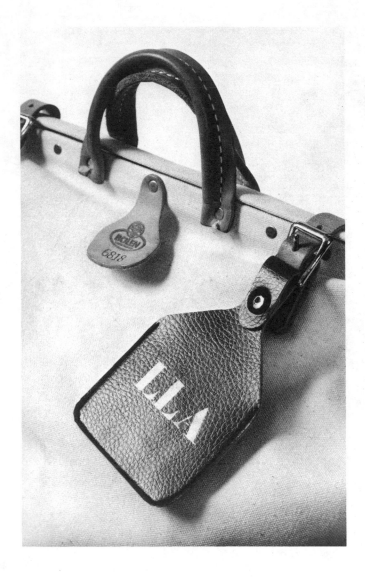

Materials: Scrap of leather, vinyl, or other sturdy fabric that needs no hemming; white acrylic paint; stencil letters (sheets from the five-and-ten); stencil brush; heavy snap; tracing paper; scissors; index card; small piece of acetate (perhaps a photo album sleeve).

Directions

Trace the letters on paper so you have a guide to follow when stenciling. In this way you can determine how closely spaced they will be. Trace the pattern outline around the letters to be sure they will fit.

Stencil initials on the fabric before cutting (see page 89 for general directions). Leave enough room all around the fabric for the tag outline.

Trace the luggage tag pattern and place the new tracing over the stenciled monogram so it is centered. Hold the tracing in position and cut out with scissors.

Note: Use a penny to draw perfectly rounded corners.

Repeat for the back piece. Write name and address on an index card. Cut out window from back piece as indicated on the pattern. Cut index card to fit inside window.

Follow the directions on snap package for attaching (see pattern for placement). With backs together, stitch front and back around side and bottom edges. This can be done on a machine or with a whipstitch for decoration.

Slip name card with piece of clear acetate over it into the window area.

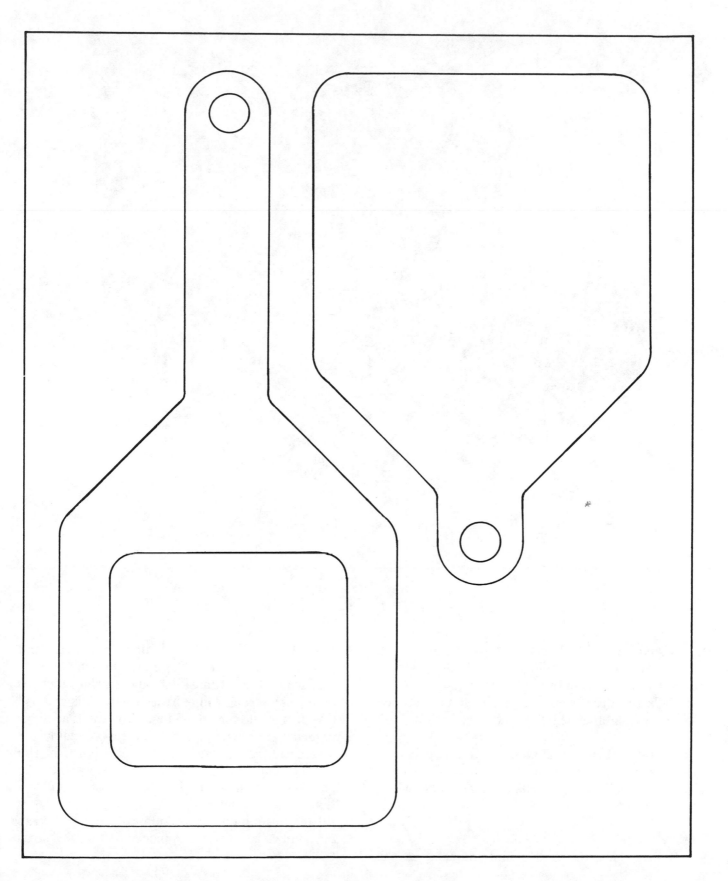

Bookend/doorstop

Make this bookend or doorstop—it can be used either way—by stenciling Naugahyde, leather, or vinyl and wrapping it around a brick. The stencils are already cut for you as you use stencil letters available in the five-and-ten.

Materials: 1 brick (available building-supply center); smooth fabric; glue; tracing paper; stencil letters; small stencil brush; small tube white acrylic paint.

Directions
Measure length, width, and diameter of the brick. Cut one long piece of fabric to wrap around all but the short ends. Cut 2 end pieces.

Place a strip of masking tape on the fabric to give you a straight line. Trace the initials and use this as a guide for stenciling. Tape the tracing at two corners of the paper. Slide the stencil letter under the tracing and get it in position. Lift the tracing and stencil letters in place with acrylic paint and small stencil brush. (For stencil directions, see page 89).

Spread glue on wrong side of fabric and wrap around brick. Attach end pieces. It's as simple as that.

You can find inexpensive lanterns that hold candles in most home-center stores. They do not have to be this exact size in order to do the project. This is a good way to decorate an existing item that you may have purchased to give as a gift. Add a little flower chain and leaves with some paint and a stencil brush.

Materials: Glass candle lantern; tracing paper; model lacquer paints in red, green, blue, white, and yellow; thinner (used for model airplanes and available in the five-and-ten); pointed artist's brush; small stencil brush; stencil paper.

Directions

Trace design on tracing paper. Cut around the design and slip paper inside glass globe. Tape lightly in position to use as a guide.

Trace design once more and tape to stencil paper. Cut out each design element. (See general how-to's on pages 16 and 89.)

Pour small amount of paint into a dish and stencil to cutout areas. Fill in flower petals, then stem and leaves. Let dry about 10 minutes and apply a second coat of paint if necessary. Unlike acrylic paint, the lacquer is washable.

Give this gift with a set of candles to match the floral design.

Fabric crafts

Fabric crafts are probably the most popular for many reasons. Most of us find sewing second nature and even a beginner can make simple straight-seam projects. For example, very easy-to-sew pillows such as those on page 104 can be made for gift giving. By selecting designer fabrics you can turn an everyday project into a boutique accessory. No further crafting skills are required. On the other hand, with the addition of an appliqué or a patchwork design you can create an extra special gift.

Fabric shops are exciting places to visit. Who among us can resist the creative urge when faced with so many incredible textures, colors, and patterns? One project pattern can be used to create a variety of gifts by simply changing fabrics, colors, and prints.

I find it most rewarding to take a flat piece of fabric and be able to turn it into a three-dimensional item. There is a certain kind of security in knowing that whenever I want to, I can reach into my fabric-filled blanket chest, sit down at the sewing machine, and turn out a handmade gift or an accessory for my home.

I haven't included clothing in this chapter because it takes more time for fitting, etc. But, in keeping with my night-before-Christmas crafting theme, anyone with a scrap of fabric, needle, and thread has all that's needed to turn out a delightful last-minute gift that won't look it.

Easy decorator pillows

Making pillows is not a new idea. In fact, throw pillows are the easiest decorative accessories to make for a room facelift. If you have some pretty scrap fabrics in your sewing basket consider this as a last-minute gift that anyone will appreciate. Add contrasting or matching welting and a contrasting backing for extra pizazz!

Materials: Enough fabric for a 12-, 14-, or 16-inch square pillow; cording to go around all sides; bias hem facing or bias strip of fabric; pillow form or polyfil stuffing.

Directions

Cut fabric for top and back to desired dimensions with ½-inch seam allowance. To make welting, open bias hem facing and fold over cording so raw edges are even. Use a zipper foot to stitch close to the cord.

For a tailored pillow you might like to make the welting from the pillow fabric. Cut bias strips of fabric wide enough to fit over the cord with an extra inch for the seam. Join strips of fabric to make a long enough strip to go all around the pillow.

With raw edges aligned and cording toward center of pillow front, pin welting all around. Stitch welting to the fabric starting 1 inch from one end. Finish sewing with 1 inch left unstitched at end.

Open stitching of both ends and cut cord so they meet. Turn one raw end of bias fabric in ½ inch and lap over other end. Stitch to pillow top.

Pin right sides of fabric together with welting between. Stitch around three sides following stitch line of welting.

Turn right side out and insert pillow form or fill with polyfil stuffing. Turn raw edges in ½ inch and slipstitch closed or add zipper to opening.

Country ruffled pillow

This country pillow is made up of one quilt block and combines two different prints for the background and borders. Two-inch-wide hem facing is used to create the pinwheel design. A wide eyelet ruffle adds to the country charm.

You can use almost any small printed fabric for this quick and easy project. The center block here is brown with small flowers in blue, yellow, and red. The border design emphasizes the blue in a small flower print. The hem facing is a good way to do appliqué without turning and hemming. Choose colors to match your fabric. Here the pinwheel is red, blue, green, and yellow. The finished size is 12 × 12 inches.

Materials: ¼ yard brown printed fabric; ⅜ yard blue fabric; tracing paper; 1 package each of green, red, blue, and yellow 2-inch-wide hem facing; 49 inches of 3-inch-wide eyelet ruffle; polyfil stuffing.

Directions

Cut a 10½ × 10½–inch square of brown fabric. Cut 2 strips of blue fabric 2½ × 12½ inches and 2 strips 2½ × 10½ inches. Cut backing square 12½ × 12½ inches.

Trace the template and transfer to cardboard. Use this to cut 1 piece each of hem facing colors.

Draw a diagonal line from corner to corner with chalk. Repeat for other corner. Pin green and blue hem facing strips along drawn lines; pin yellow and red against opposite line. Slide the cut ends underneath the first 2 strips. Machine stitch all hem facing pieces on the quilt square.

With right sides facing, pin one short border strip to the top of center square. Attach bottom strip. Stitch across, leaving ¼-inch seam. Pin long strips to either side of square and stitch. Open seams and press.

Ruffle

To make the eyelet ruffle, seam ends of strip together to form a loop. Divide eyelet into fourths and mark with pins. Evenly distribute ruffle around edge of pillow, pinning right sides together (see diagram). Stitch around.

With right sides facing, pin backing to pillow front with ruffled eyelet between. Stitch around 3 sides. Turn right side out and stuff. Close opening with a slipstitch.

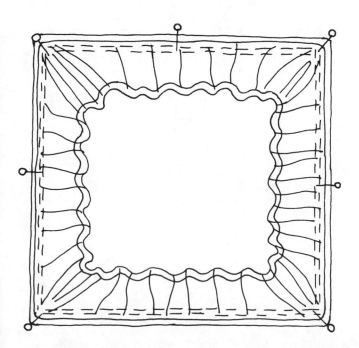

Template for country pillow

Baby pillow

This little gingham pillow is 11 × 11 inches and fits nicely into a carriage or crib. It's easy to make and you can add a cross-stitch saying or design because the gingham squares are perfect for this (see page 43). Add the baby's name and birth date for a new parent to cherish.

Materials: ½ yard yellow gingham fabric (smallest check); 1½ yards eyelet ruffle; 1½ yards ribbon eyelet; 1½ yards of ¼-inch orange satin ribbon; polyfil stuffing.

Directions

Cut 2 pieces of gingham 12 × 12 inches. With right edges facing stitch ends of ruffle together to form a loop. Divide into fours and pin evenly around front of one piece of fabric. Edge of ruffle should align with raw edge of fabric. Machine baste. Turn ruffle up.

Thread ¼-inch ribbon through the ribbon eyelet and stitch in place on the pillow where the ruffle eyelet meets the fabric. Be sure that ends of ribbon start and stop at the top center, leaving enough to tie a bow.

Fold outside ruffle toward center again (over the ribbon eyelet). With right sides facing, pin the pillow back to the top, with ruffle between. Stitch around 3 sides, leaving an opening for turning. Trim corners, turn right side out, and stuff. Slipstitch closed.

Note: If adding cross-stitch, do this before any sewing. Use the right side of one pillow square. Be sure to center the design correctly.

Patchwork stocking and ornament

Gather all your scrap pieces of fabric together to make a brightly colored Christmas stocking from odds and ends. And then with the smallest pieces you can make a little stocking ornament to fill with candy canes or to hang by the fireplace for the family pet.

Materials for patchwork stocking: 97 squares of a variety of fabrics, $1\frac{1}{2} \times 1\frac{1}{2}$ inches; $1\frac{1}{2}$ yards eyelet or lace; $1\frac{1}{2}$ yards of $\frac{1}{4}$-inch satin ribbon; $1\frac{1}{2}$ yards of $\frac{1}{2}$-inch grosgrain ribbon; backing piece of fabric (such as felt or printed cotton), $9\frac{1}{2} \times 14\frac{1}{2}$ inches.

Directions

Begin by enlarging the stocking pattern.

To make the patchwork design, cut fabric pieces into $1\frac{1}{2} \times 1\frac{1}{2}$–inch squares. Select a variety of fabrics that will look good together. For a country classic choose calico or bright Christmas material. If you are using two or three different fabrics, cut equal amounts of each. There are so many variations you can create for this project that I'm sure you'll want to take the time to decide what color scheme you'd like best.

Follow the diagram and sew vertical rows together with $\frac{1}{2}$-inch seam allowance in the following way: 2 rows of 13 squares, 4 rows of 14 squares each, 1 row of 6, 2 rows of 5.

Beginning with the heel side, place row 2 on top of row 1 with right sides facing and raw edges aligned. Stitch together on right-hand edge. Open flat and press.

Continue to stitch rows together in this way. When all 9 rows are joined you can cut out stocking shape.

Place tracing pattern over patch pieces and pin. Cut out stocking shape. Cut another stocking from the backing material. There will be a $\frac{1}{2}$-inch seam allowance all around.

With right sides facing and raw edges aligned, pin eyelet around outside edge of patched piece beginning at top of left edge and ending on opposite side. Do not extend lace across top. Machine baste.

With right sides facing, pin backing to front of stocking and stitch together leaving top open. Turn right side out. Fold top raw edge to inside $\frac{1}{4}$ inch and press. Turn down another $\frac{1}{4}$ inch and stitch around.

Add ribbon all around stocking and across front of top approximately 1 inch down from top. Tie ribbon bow in front if desired. Add ribbon loop to corner of edge opening.

Materials for stocking ornament: 40 squares of fabric, $1\frac{1}{2} \times 1\frac{1}{2}$ inches; backing fabric, 6×8 inches; eyelet and ribbons if desired (22 inches of each).

Directions

You can make this little stocking ornament from a few leftovers to match the larger stocking or it can be completely different.

Make this as you did the larger stocking. Stitch vertical rows of fabric together in the following way: 1 row of 7 squares, 3 rows of 8, 1 row of 5, 4 rows of 4.

Cut out front and back using the stocking pattern provided same size here. No enlarging is necessary. Finish as with other project. Add ribbon and lace as before.

Patchwork stocking and ornament

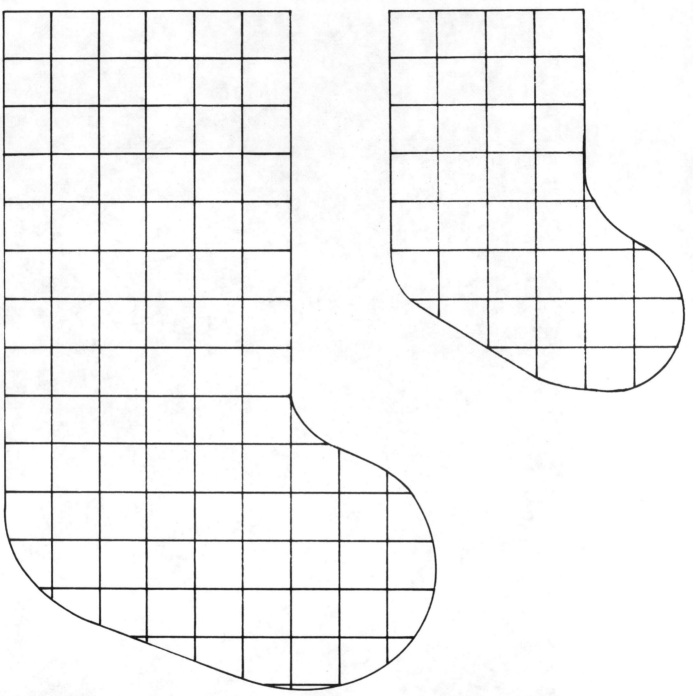

Each square equals 1".

This Christmas wreath patchwork pillow will be most appreciated for holiday spruce-up in any home. You can make it with white and green printed fabric. The center is made with red Aida even-weave fabric so you can cross-stitch the message on it. (See page 43 for easy cross-stitch directions.) The finished size is 14 × 14 inches.

Materials: ½ yard fabric A; ½ yard fabric B; 6½-inch square of red 12-count Aida cloth; 1 skein white embroidery floss; embroidery hoop; needle; solid fabric for backing; polyfil stuffing; ½ yard of 2-inch-wide red ribbon.

Directions

Cut 2 6½-inch squares from fabric A. Cut 2 6½-inch squares from fabric B. Fold all fabric squares on the diagonal and cut on the line. You now have 4 triangles of each fabric.

Refer to the piecing diagram and with right sides facing stitch A and B triangles together with ½-inch seam allowance. Press all seams on back of patched piece.

Cross-stitch

Center letters on Aida cloth and follow chart to do cross-stitch. (See general directions on page 43.)

Finish

Place patched piece over red Aida and adjust so the word is centered. Pin in place and stitch around edge by hand or on the machine with same color thread.

Use this as your pattern for the back and pin to backing fabric. Cut around outside edge. If you want to add piping to the outside rim, see page 104 for complete directions.

With right sides facing, stitch around all edges with a ½-inch seam allowance. Leave one side of octagonal shape open for turning. Turn to right side and stuff with polyfil. Close top with slip-stitch.

Make a ribbon bow and tack to top of pillow.

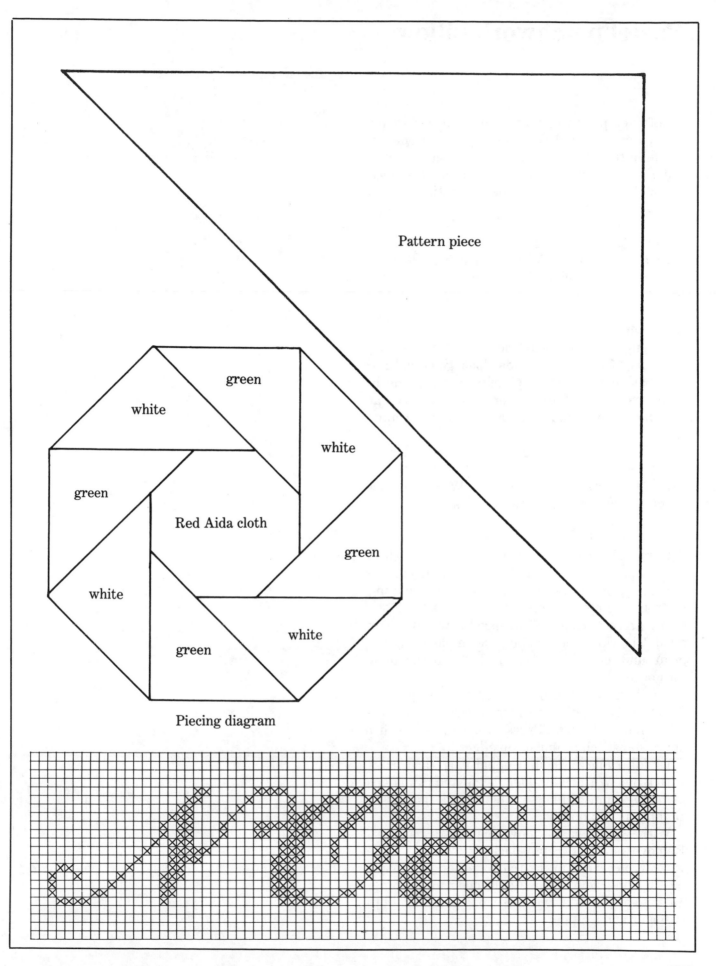

Pattern piece

Piecing diagram

Pastel patchwork pillow

Leftover pieces of pastel chintz are used for this patchwork pillow. The ruffle is made by stitching together several strips of each color to make a piece long enough to go around a 16-inch pillow form. Thus, the ruffle is multicolored to match the 9-patch design.

Materials: 9 squares of fabric, 5¾ inches (¼-inch seam allowance); fabric strip for ruffle, 4½ × 96 inches; 16-inch pillow form; fabric for backing, 16½ × 16½ inches.

Directions

Arrange squares of fabric so that colors (and patterns, if not using solids) look good and are well balanced. For this pillow I used a blue in each corner, a pink in the center with a green at top and bottom, and lavender squares at center sides.

With right sides facing and raw edges aligned, stitch across one edge. Open and press. Make 3 rows of 3 patches in this way. With rows arranged, attach as for single patches.

Ruffle

Using all 4 colors, cut equal lengths of each to total approximately 96 inches. If you don't have enough of one color to equal another it doesn't matter. The effect is one of a rainbow and if the colors are not perfectly balanced it will still look good. The ruffle piece should be ample enough to go around the pillow one and a half times to allow for gathers.

Stitch pieces together to make one long strip. Stitch ends together to form a circle. Turn one edge under ¼ inch. Press. Turn under ¼ inch again and stitch to finish top edge.

Divide ruffle strip in 4 equal parts and mark with a pin. With right sides facing and raw edges matching, pin ruffle to pillow top, gathering slightly as you do this.

With ½-inch seam allowance, baste together. Remove pins and repin backing over the ruffle with wrong side up. Stitch together just inside basting line, leaving one side open for turning. Turn to right side and close opening with slip-stitch or add a zipper.

No-sew poppy pillow

Brighten any room with this no-sew, floral appliqué pillow. With little or no experience you can make this decorative oversized pillow or the following matching project, on page 124.

Traditionally, appliqué involves cutting, piecing, and stitching. But I've taken the work out of it with a simplified technique. Just cut the large flowers from colorful cotton-blend fabric. Apply to any background material with fusible webbing. Use marking pens to add detail or a few stitches for interest. It's as easy as that: The finished size is 14 × 14 inches.

Materials: ⅝ yard unbleached muslin; colorful cotton fabric as indicated on pattern; Stacy's Stitch Witchery (available in fabric stores by the yard); polyfil stuffing (1½ pounds per pillow); markers (optional).

Directions

Enlarge appliqué pattern pieces on tracing paper (see page 14). Pin tracing paper patterns to fabric and Stitch Witchery and cut out each piece. You will have a double piece (fabric and fusible webbing) for each design element.

Cut 2 pieces of muslin, 16 × 16 inches. Follow design layout and place each piece on one piece of muslin. Repin these elements here and there to hold in place. Fuse to muslin with a hot iron (see directions on package).

Stitch around leaves and flowers if desired. Stitching is not necessary, however, to hold the appliqués in place. Use waterproof markers to add detail or use black thread and machine stitch details.

Place second piece of muslin over front piece and stitch around, leaving ½-inch seam allowance. Leave enough of an opening on one side to turn pillow right side out.

Trim seams, press, and turn to right side. Fill with polyfil until pillow is packed and very full. Stitch opening closed.

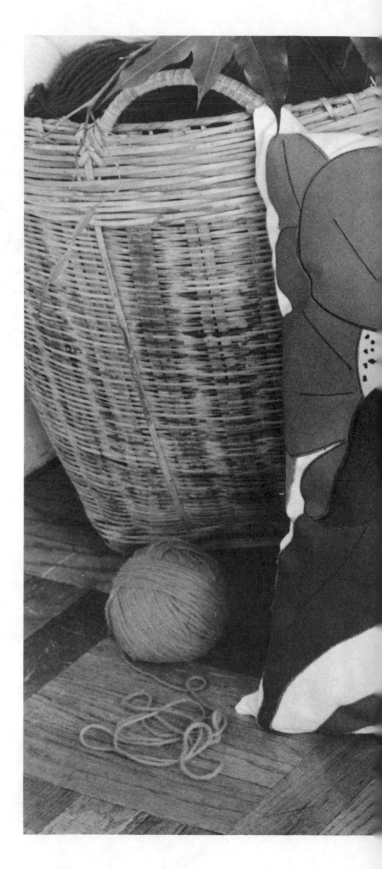

Left lower quarter

Left upper quarter

Ruffled appliqué tablecloth

The appliqués are applied with fusible web. You can make a new tablecloth or spruce up an old one with these oversized poppy blossoms. For general directions, see page 15. The tablecloth is made for a 42-inch round table. Adjust length for different size tables.

Materials: 6 yards of 45-inch-wide fabric (Laura Ashley's "Poppy" is used here); colored fabrics for appliqués; Stitch Witchery; 9 yards of 1-inch-wide red bias tape; 3 yards of ½-inch-wide red bias tape; 9 yards of 7-inch eyelet (Wm. E. Wright Co. eyelet is used here).

Directions

Tablecloth

Cut 6 yards of fabric in half lengthwise. Cut one of the 3-yard pieces in half lengthwise.

Sew each narrow piece to either side edge of the 45-inch-wide piece to create a seam at each side.

Find the center of the fabric. Attach a long string to the end of a pencil. Pin end of string to center of cloth (or have another person hold it there) and bring pencil end to edge of fabric.

Draw a wide circle by swinging the pencil around the fabric. Cut off excess material by cutting along penciled circle line.

Position fabric on your table and pin eyelet to edge of fabric approximately 1 inch up from raw edge (adjust for drop from tabletop to floor on your table). Stitch around. Add 1-inch bias tape over eyelet edge where it joins the fabric.

Appliqués

Enlarge poppy patterns and leaf pieces (see page 14). Use the poppy pattern on page 121. Transfer to tracing paper. Cut out each pattern piece and pin to fabric and fusible web, following color key.

Pin appliqués around tablecloth so they are nicely spaced. You can add leaves where they look best (see photo of design layout). Fuse appliqués in place with hot iron. For added detail and strength you can stitch around each piece with a zigzag stitch in the color of the fabric.

Place tablecloth back on table and pin ½-inch bias tape around top edge of tablecloth. This is done last to be sure of the placement of the tape in relation to the appliqués. Stitch around.

You can also add an extra appliqué to the center of the top if desired.

Leaf pattern

Leaf patterns

This is one of the easiest craft projects in the book and one that will surely make all your gifts look special. While they are designed as gift tags you can make them as Christmas ornaments and in no time you can fill your tree with a variety of shapes and colors. Choose small printed fabrics and get the children in on the act. This is an assembly-line project.

Materials: A variety of fabrics; fusible web such as Stacy's Stitch Witchery; interfacing; scissors; tracing paper; paper punch; ribbons for hanging or tying on gifts.

Directions

Each ornament or tag is a different shape and can be made with one fabric for one side and another for the reverse side. It's a good way to use your scrap fabrics.

Place one piece of fabric on a flat surface wrong side up. On top of this place a piece of fusible web, over which goes a piece of interfacing, followed by another piece of fusible web and another printed fabric face up. Using a hot iron, fuse all materials together.

Trace each pattern and pin to the fabric. Or, if it is too thick to insert a pin easily, make a cardboard template of the patterns and lay them on the fabric. Then draw around each. Cut each shape out, punch a hole in the top, thread a ribbon loop through, and that's it.

129

Knitting

The following are small and easy projects to make from leftover yarns. The vest is a large item but is worked on #9 needles, which makes it a quick project for its size.

Note for beginners: Knitting depends on learning how to do two basic stitches, knit (k) and purl (p). With these you can make all kinds of projects.

With the basic knit and purl stitch you can produce what is known as a stockinette pattern. This is the most popular stitch combination, and is easy to learn. If you're a beginner you'll have no trouble. An experienced knitter will find these projects a snap.

You'll find the basic embroidery stitch guide on page 18 helpful when adding the embroidered flower chain to the vest.

Bunny slippers

Make these bunny slippers for your favorite wee one. The big floppy pink ears will delight any child. Since the slippers look best when made of white yarn I've used washable acrylic. When they get dirty, they can be simply tossed in the washer.

The slippers can be made to fit size 2–4. Directions for sizes 4–6 and 6–8 are given in parentheses.

Materials: 4 ozs. white knitting worsted-weight acrylic yarn; small amount of pink yarn same weight; 2 black buttons for eyes (eyes could also be embroidered); carpet thread; needle.

Needle: #9

Gauge: 4 sts = 1 inch

6 rows = 1-inch garter stitch (all knit)

Directions

Use double strand of yarn and cast on 29 (35) (41) sts.

Row 1: All knit.

Row 2: K 9 (11) (13), * p 1, k 9 (11) (13), repeat from * once more.

Repeat rows 1 and 2 until there are 13 (16) (19) garter stitch ridges on right side, ending with row 2.

Shape toe

Row 1: P 1, * k 1, p 1, repeat from * across row.

Row 2: K 1, * p 1, k 1, repeat from * across row.

Repeat these 2 rows 3 (5) (7) times more, then work row 1 once more.

Break off yarn, leaving an 8-inch end.

Draw end thru remaining sts and pull up tightly.

Sew ribbing edges tog to form toe. Fold the cast-on edge in half and seam for center back.

Ears

Make 4. With white single strand cast on 7 sts. Work 8 rows in stockinette st.

Next row: K 2 tog, k 3, k 2 tog.

Next row: Purl.

Next row: K 2 tog, k 1, k 2 tog.

Break off yarn. Leave an 8-inch end. Pull end thru sts and draw up tightly.

Repeat to make 4 pieces with pink yarn.

With pink piece in front of white, overcast around edges with white yarn to join front and back of ears. Place in position on front of each slipper and stitch together. Sew buttons in front of each ear with carpet thread so child cannot easily pull buttons off (see diagram for placement). With pink, embroider nose over front hole using satin stitch (see stitch guide, page 18).

Whiskers

With 6-inch-long carpet thread, insert thru from one side of front hole on toe to other. Repeat twice more.

Pompom tail

Wrap white yarn around your hand about 24 times. Slide off and tie a piece of yarn around the middle to hold bundle together. Cut off ends of loops and fluff into a ball. Trim if necessary. Repeat. Stitch to back of each slipper.

Embroidered vest

This vest is made with washable knitting worsted and takes three 3-oz. skeins for small, medium, or large. You will have some left over on the small and medium.

The embroidery is easy to add with the use of a product called Trace Erase from Stacy. This is a gauzelike paper used for tracing the design. You pin it in position on your knit background and embroider right through it. In this way you can follow the exact lines of petals and leaves, stems and buds. When finished, the paper is easy to pull away from the yarn and leaves a perfect design.

Materials: 3 skeins (3 oz. each) Bucilla Wonderknit knitting worsted in ecru; darning needle; 1–2–3 ply Persian-type yarn—1 skein each of blue and yellow and 3 skeins each of pink and green; Trace Erase.
Needles: #7 and #9
Crochet hook: I—for edging and ties (optional)
Gauge: 3 sts = 1 inch
        6 rows = 1 inch

Directions

All directions are for S (32–34); those for M (36–38) and L (40–42) are given in parentheses.

Back

With #7 needles cast on 68 (74) (80) stitches. Work 6 rows in garter stitch (all knit). Change to #9 needles and work in stockinette st (knit 1 row, purl 1 row) until piece measures 10 inches.

Shape armhole

At beginning of each of next 2 rows bind off 7 sts. Decrease 1 st each end of needle every 3 times. Work even on 48 (54) (60) sts until armholes measure 7½ (8¼) (8½) inches.

Shape neck

K 12 (14) (16) sts. Join another ball of yarn and bind off center 24 (26) (28) sts. Knit to end of row. Working on both sides at once, k 1 row.

Shape shoulders

At each arm edge bind off 12 (14) (16) sts.

Left front

With #7 needles cast on 34 (37) (40) sts. Work 6 rows in garter stitch. Change to #9 needles and work in stockinette st until piece measures 10 inches.

Shape arm and neck

At beginning of next row bind off 7 sts. Work to end of row. At beg of next row (neck edge), decrease 1 st at the end of needle (armhole) every fourth row 3 times. Continue decreasing at neck edge until there are 12 (14) (16) sts.

Work even on 12 (14) (16) sts until armhole measures 7½ (8¼) (8½) inches. Bind off.

Right front

Work to correspond to left front reversing all shaping.

Finishing

Sew shoulders together with a blunt darning needle. With right sides together and edges matching, overcast the yarn on both pieces. Do not pull yarn too taut. Weave yarn end into seam stitches. Do not knot.

Armhole edge

Open flat. Using #7 needles with right sides facing, pick up 50 (54) (58) sts and work 5 rows in garter st. Bind off loosely. Sew underarm. Work single row of crochet around left side, neck, and right side edges. Fasten off.

Ties (to be crocheted)

Make 2. With crochet hook chain 40. Draw up last loop 2 inches long. Insert hook in 2nd ch from hook and draw up a loop 2 inches. Break off end leaving a 2-inch end. Knot below last chain. Snip ends to make tassels. Sew each tie to opposite edges of front neck opening.

Embroidery

Enlarge design (see page 14). Place Trace Erase over tracing, leaving enough room to trace the design twice. Trace on one side, then turn Trace Erase over and repeat. Cut apart so you have 2 separate tracings for either side of front of vest. Pin in position along front edges of vest.

Work over the traced design. Using green yarn, backstitch to create the vine all around front of vest edge. Follow the outline and fill in leaf areas with satin stitch. Use pink yarn to fill in flower petals; fill centers of flowers with yellow. With blue, work buds in satin stitch. Weave ends of yarn under existing stitches on underside of vest.

To remove excess paper, snip around designs and pull stubborn pieces out from under embroidery with tweezers.

Finish

Pad ironing board and press on wrong side of vest with a warm steam iron. While slightly damp, block vest to shape.

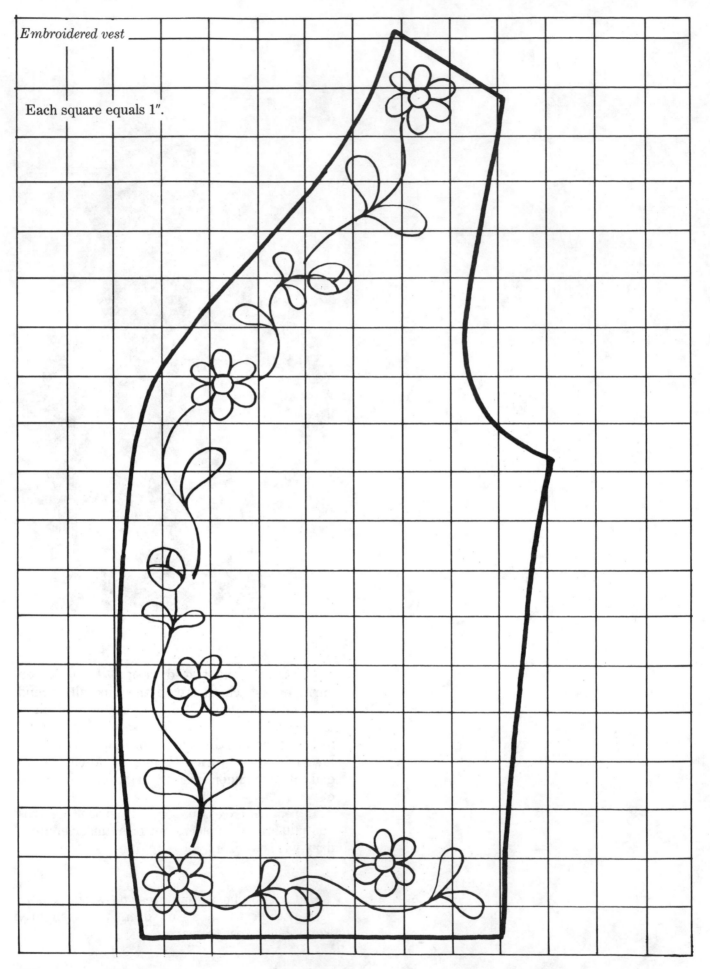

Embroidered vest

Each square equals 1″.

What small child wouldn't love to wear these puppy mittens with their floppy ears? These are made with bright yellow acrylic, a washable yarn, but you might like to make brown puppies or another bright un-puppy color like red. The face shows up best on a bright, light color. Instructions are for S (2–4) M (6–8), and L (10–12).

Materials: 2-oz. ball yellow knitting worsted yarn; 1 skein each of black and red embroidery floss; embroidery needle; Trace Erase.
Needles: #4 and #6
Gauge: 5 sts = 1 inch
    7 rows = 1 inch

Directions

Right mitten

Using #4 needles, cast on 30 (36) (40) sts. K 1, p 1 in ribbing for 2 (2) (2½) inches. Change to #6 needles and work in stockinette st (k 1 row, p 1 row) for 4 (4) (6) rows.

Shape thumb gusset
Row 1: K 14 (17) (19) sts, put a marker on the needle, inc 1 st in each of next 2 sts, put a marker on needle, k 14 (17) (19) sts.
Row 2 and all even rows: Purl. Be sure to slip the markers onto the right needle each time you come to them.
Row 3: K to first marker, inc 1 st in next st, k to 1 st before 2nd marker, inc 1 st in next st, k to end of row.
    Repeat rows 2 and 3 until there are 8 (10) (12) sts between markers, ending with a p row.
Row 7 (9) (11): K to first marker, sl these knitted 14 (17) (19) sts onto a holder, k to next marker, turn, sl remaining 14 (17) (19) sts onto another holder.

Thumb

Working on 8 (10) (12) sts, at beg of each of next 2 rows cast on 1 st. Work even rows in stockinette st on 10 (12) (14) sts until piece measures desired finished length, ending with a p row.

Shape top

K 2 tog across row. Break off yarn, leaving a 12-inch end. Pull end through 5 (6) (7) sts and draw up tightly. Sew seam.

Hand

Sl 14 (17) (19) sts onto larger needles (#6), join yarn at start of thumb and pick up 2 sts over thumb, k 14 (17) (19) sts from second holder onto same needle. Work even in stockinette st on 30 (36) (40) sts until piece measures 1½ inches less than desired finished length, ending with a p row.

Shape top

Row 1: *K 2 tog, k 4 (4) (6) sts, repeat from * to end of row.
Row 2 and all even rows: Purl.
Row 3: *K 2 tog, k 3 (3) (5) sts, repeat from * to end of row.

Continue in this manner to dec 5 (6) (5) sts every other row until 5 (6) (5) sts remain. Break off yarn, leaving a 12-inch end. Finish in same way as top of thumb.

Left Mitten

Work same as right mitten.

Ears

Make 4. Cast on 14 sts. Work 10 rows in stockinette st (k 1 row, p 1 row).
Next row: K 2 tog, k 3, k 2 tog, k 2 tog, k 3, k 2 tog.
Next row: Purl.
Next row: K 2 tog, k 1, k 2 tog, k 2 tog, k 1, k 2 tog.

Break off yarn, leaving an 8-inch end. Pull end through sts and draw up tightly. Sew seam.

Place in position on front of each mitten and stitch together.

Face

Trace doggy face on Trace Erase and pin to front of each mitten. Using black floss work a running stitch for outline of face. Satin stitch the eyes and nose. Use red floss and a satin stitch for the tongue.

Calligraphy

Calligraphy is elegant handwriting that is often used for special occasions such as to address wedding invitations. It adds the perfect finishing touch to holiday projects.

Calligraphy basics are easy to learn and anyone can become proficient enough to produce professional-looking results with a little practice. The tools are few and with the chisel-point markers suggested in this chapter, colorful results can be achieved as well as the traditional black lettering.

By its nature, calligraphy adds a very personal quality to a gift, an invitation, or a poem to be framed.

There are many styles of lettering in calligraphy. They were developed over many centuries and in many languages. The Italic alphabet presented here is the closest to normal handwriting and, therefore, one of the easiest to learn.

Basic directions

Refer to the alphabet on the facing page and note that the letters all lean to the right. This is called the slant. It should not be confused with the pen angle.

Pen angle: Italic calligraphy is rendered at a 45° angle. This means that the relationship of the pen nib to the vertical and horizontal lines on a piece of paper is 45°. It does not refer to your arm, your hand, or the tilt of the pen (see pen angle diagram). By maintaining the 45° angle, the special characteristics of Italic will be achieved. Other letter styles have different pen angles.

Practice

In order to get used to both slant and pen angle, practice on graph paper so you can clearly see the verticals and horizontals from which you are calculating angles. After a little practice you will "feel" the rhythm of Italic calligraphy and it will start to flow easily.

As guides for letter height, rule lines lightly in pencil.

Letter height

The height of a letter is related to the width of the pen nib used. For example, capital letters are 7 nib-widths high. For lower case, the body of the letter is 5 nib widths; the ascenders and descenders are 2 nib widths (see diagram).

When ruling your guidelines be sure to determine the desired distance between lines.

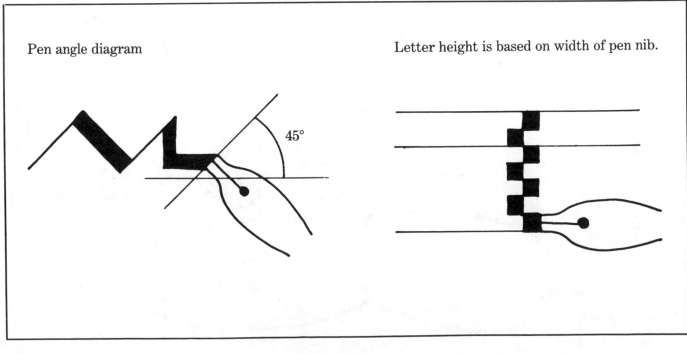

Pen angle diagram

45°

Letter height is based on width of pen nib.

Italic alphabet

a b c d e f g h i j k l m n

o p q r s t u v w x y z

A B C D E F G H I J

K L M N O P Q R

S T U V W X Y Z

1 2 3 4 5 6 7 8 9 0

Stationery and envelope

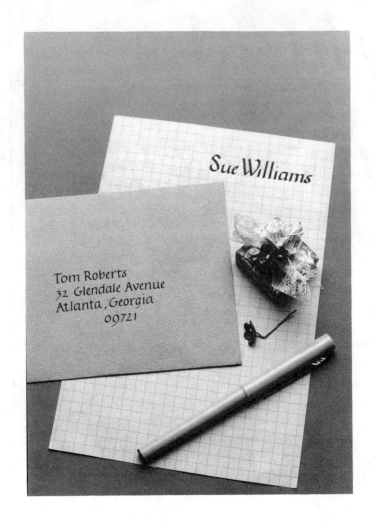

There are many styles of unprinted stationery available for an enterprising calligrapher. The grid paper in this project is easy to use for calligraphy and is a good way to get started. The contrasting envelope adds interest.

Materials: Stationery and envelope; calligraphy pen; ink; 2H pencil; ruler; T-square; scrap of paper.

Directions

Use the scrap of paper to lay out your letterhead and envelope. When you have the desired spacing, rule lines on the envelope and letterhead to the correct letter size.

Before doing the envelope, practice a few times to get used to the flow. Then do the envelope at the same pace that was comfortable when practicing. If you have a group of envelopes to do, do them one after the other. They will get better and better. Calligraphy is a spontaneous process and shouldn't be labored.

Follow the same procedure for the letterhead. If you are making a large letter form as in the example shown here, remember to use a nib that is appropriate for the size of letters. After lettering the words erase lines.

You can use a purchased invitation as a starting point for your calligraphic invitation. Plan your design first on a scrap of paper to be sure the layout is the way you want it. The invitation shown here has all the lines centered to the right and left. To get everything centered just right, try your entire invitation on scrap paper and do it over a few times until you get each line in the right place.

Materials: Invitation cards and envelopes; pen; ink; scrap paper.

Directions

Rule lines on all the invitations and letter them in. Follow the same steps for the envelopes.

If you are having a large party and want to have your own design printed rather than doing them by hand, it is easy to prepare.

For printing you will need these additional materials: nonreproducing blue pencil (from an art store) and black ink.

Once you have arrived at the final layout, rule the guide lines in blue on good paper. Do the calligraphy in black. Draw the outline of the invitation in blue around the lettering so the printer will have the correct position. (Before giving your invitation to the printer, recheck time, date, and spelling.)

Place cards, labels, tags

Place cards can be done easily on a large sheet of bristol board. Just rule long guidelines for the names and leave enough space between rows of guidelines to accommodate the flaps that fold over to make the place card. By doing the names on a large sheet, you can center them easily before cutting out each place card. Any decorative paper can be used as the material for a place card.

Labels can be made from standard labels as shown here. The border is red, the letters bright blue. As with place cards, almost any pretty paper can make a good background for a label.

Giftwrapping

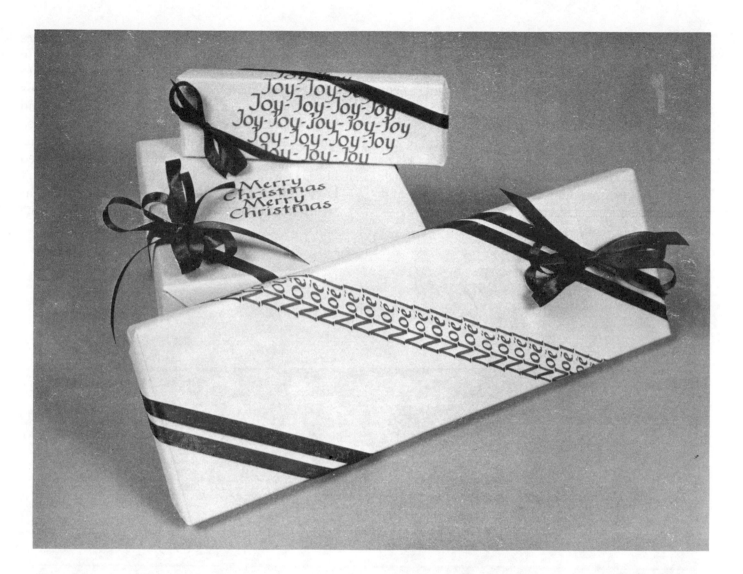

Calligraphy can be used to create designs and patterns of letters and words. These examples are just a few of the ways to create handcrafted gift wraps. They were created with red and green chisel-point markers, which are available in art supply and stationery stores.

These designs were a result of experimenting on scrap paper. Use them or create your own. Once your design is determined, rule the lines on the gift wrap paper and letter your words in the colors of your choice.

Choose ribbons to match and plan your placement to best go with the calligraphy.

Treasures from throwaways

Whether it's egg cartons, plastic detergent bottles, corrugated boxes, glass bottles, jars, or soda cans, there's a treasure trove in all that trash. The trick is to make them look more like treasure than what they are.

Most craftworkers welcome ideas and how-to's for using everyday free objects. This chapter will give you some practical, clever, and pretty ways to do this. In our economy-conscious era such projects are appealing for both gift giving and bazaar sales.

So begin collecting your garbage long before Christmas. Wash out cans, remove labels from bottles, smooth out wrinkled wrapping paper (a slightly warm iron helps), collect odds and ends of buttons, lace, and ribbons for trimmings, and look at everything with a creative eye. You'll be surprised how many things you'll think of on your own once you make a few of the projects offered here. It will prove to you that Christmas doesn't have to be a costly affair. You can give gifts that really look like they were purchased in fine stores.

Band-aid boxes

Candy can

Decoupage cans, tins, boxes, and other castoffs

Decoupage is the eighteenth-century French craft of applied cutouts. A cutout paper design is applied to a painted surface and then submerged under many coats of varnish. This is an elegant way to make throwaway tins like Band-Aid boxes and cookie containers look positively beautiful. Some of the designs are cut from wrapping paper, some from greeting cards. The designs can be glued to the outside of a box or underneath the top lid as with the plastic boxes. Elmer's Glue-All dries clear and can be applied to the front of the design, then adhered from inside. The inside is then given a coat of spray paint, which shows through the clear plastic.

Materials: Variety of tins and boxes; acrylic paint; 1-inch brush; white glue; sponge; small scissors; variety of paper designs to cut out; clear spray varnish; trimmings.

Directions

Give each item 2 or 3 coats of paint. Cut out paper designs and arrange on your items. Glue in place, wiping away excess glue with a damp sponge as you work. Let dry.

Give entire surface a coat of spray varnish. Let dry and repeat several times until surface is well coated. Add trimmings and ribbons where desired.

Coffee cans

Cover an ordinary coffee can with pretty pastel paper. Add a lace doily, some cutout flowers, ribbon, or braid trim. Cover the lid inside and out. Spray a coat of varnish over all surfaces. You can line the inside as well. Glue gold rickrack around rim of lid. Add a knob to center of lid.

Gift box

Coffee can

Paint bucket

Food containers

Candy cans

Sometimes candy comes in silver cans that almost look like real silver. When decorated with pastel flowers like these pink tulips, cut from everyday wrapping paper, these cans are wonderful for holding flowers, pencils, or letters. The decoupage process is the same as with the other projects. However, when spray varnishing try to hold the can at a distance that will allow you to evenly cover without drip marks. They will show up more strongly on a surface that isn't painted.

Plastic food containers

Throwaway plastic self hinged containers can be recycled for many uses. Cut out bright paper designs such as red tulips, pink roses, or yellow daffodils. Arrange them on top of lid to be sure they'll fit. Trim if necessary.

Spread white glue on the *front* of each flower. Glue to inside of top lid. Press firmly in place and leave to dry for an hour. When dry the glue will be clear. Spray paint entire inside of top and bottom. White paint is used here but you can use any color that is a good background for the flowers used. Attach a loop of ribbon to front with a few stitches (needle goes through the plastic). This is a little handle to pull the lid open easily.

Band-aid boxes

Paint Band-Aid tins inside and out with two different paint colors. Cut out large flowers to fill surfaces and glue all over, front, top, and sides. Coat with spray varnish. These make delightful little travel sewing kits.

Candy tins

Candy tins

Paint a candy tin in a soft country rose color. Cut out one big beautiful flower like a peony or rose to fill the top of the lid. Sometimes small spriggy flowers look best and sometimes a large flower to fill the area is exciting. Glue to top so that leaves sprawl over edges. Trim with a razor blade.

Add a wide band of lace all around bottom portion in a similar color for a subtle and elegant effect. In this case, the colors all blend rather than contrast. This would make a nice container in the bedroom for holding cosmetics, cotton balls, or sewing notions.

Gift boxes

Enhance a plain gift box with cutout flowers glued on all sides. Add 1-inch velvet ribbon and a band of lace to top lid. Cut out and glue paper flowers to top of box. Spray several coats of varnish over all paper areas. Use it to hold a gift. It might also make a nice addition to your closet for holding odds and ends.

Paint buckets

Paper paint buckets are good for holding almost anything from plants to sewing odds and ends. They are inexpensive and come in two or three sizes at a paint store. Paint outside one color, inside another. The colors should complement the cutout flowers to be glued over it. Add a rim of gold braid glued all around top and a band of lace around the top of inside. Spray varnish outside.

Wine-box cassette holder

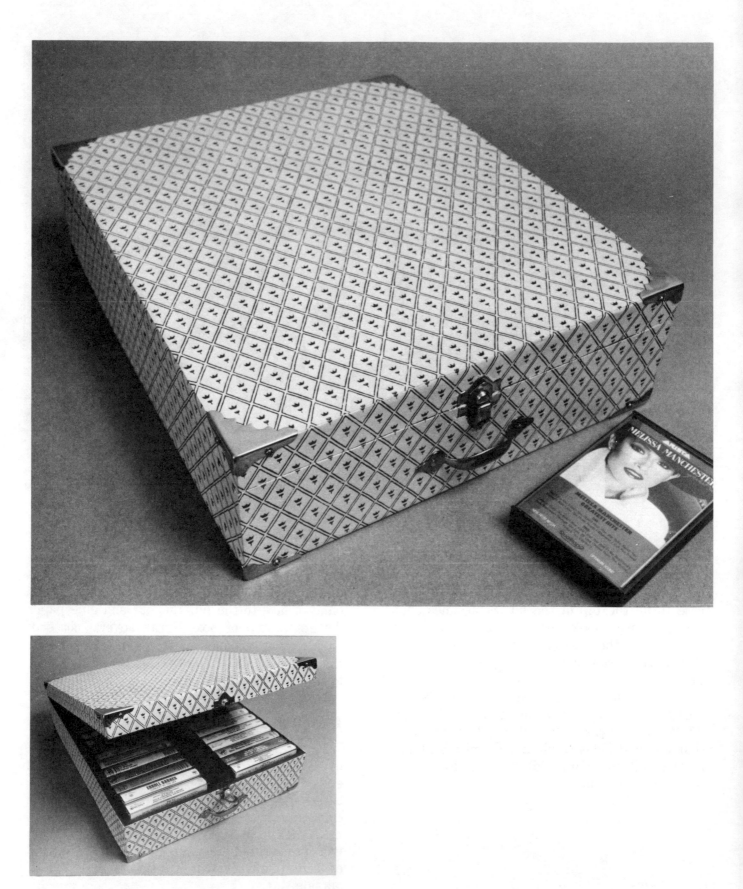

Inexpensive wine often comes in a wooden gift box that holds three or four bottles. The box, which has a clasp and handle, makes a convenient tape cassette carrier. The inside can be compartmented with strips of balsa wood inserted to fit the number of tapes.

The outside of the box can be painted, stenciled, or covered with fabric or paper. Here it is covered with a pretty wallcovering print. Choose the covering most appropriate for the person you'll be giving it to.

Materials: Wooden box; enough paper for box size; rubber cement or glue; rubber cement thinner; straightedge; razor blade; 1/8-inch balsa wood; spray paint in color to match paper; clear spray varnish; brass corners; brass handle to replace existing rope handle.

Directions

This box is 10½ × 12 inches. The center divider is made from one strip of 1/8-inch balsa cut up and glued together. Make a box of balsa to fit in center, dividing box in half lengthwise. Glue the pieces together and hold with pins while drying. Glue separator in position. Since not all boxes are the same size, you will make this divider to fit your box.

Paint inside of top edges and inside bottom. Leave inside of top unpainted.

Covering box

Measure around back, sides, and front of box. Cut a strip of paper 2 inches wider than the height and 2 inches longer than the circumference. Glue to box. Rubber cement is often used in place of glue because it is easier to redo any errors that may occur. If using rubber cement dry mount in the following way:

1. Spread rubber cement over surface of box to be covered. Set aside to dry.
2. Spread rubber cement on strip of paper and let dry.
3. Wrap strip of paper around box so that ends meet at the back. Trim extra paper from back overlap. Trim around clasp with a craft knife, razor blade, or small scissors.
4. Clip in at corners and fold top tabs over box

top (lid). Fold bottom tabs under box.
5. With a razor blade slice through opening (where top and bottom meet). Open lid and trim any excess paper.
6. Cut a piece of paper to fit top of box and another to fit the bottom of box. Dry mount.

Finish

Give all surfaces a coat of clear spray varnish to protect the paper. Add brass corners for decoration and a handle to the front.

Note: If you make an error, do not try to pull the paper away. Apply rubber cement thinner over the paper and slowly remove. Let dry and reapply the rubber cement. The paper will be as good as new.

You can add a label to the center of the top of the box for identification. See the calligraphy section on pages 140–41 and letter the person's name or initials in the center of the label.

You might even consider enclosing a tape or two to give with this gift.

Christmas basket centerpiece

Cover an oversized mushroom basket with fabric, add some eyelet and ribbon, and fill it with Christmas balls or holly for a decorative centerpiece. These baskets come in two or three sizes. If your supermarket doesn't have empty ones and you have the time, you can order them from our mail order source (see page 160).

This oversized mushroom basket is shown ready for the holidays but it can have many uses—perhaps filled with bathroom accessories, such as finger towels. Choose pastel fabric and 3-inch-wide eyelet to make a pretty object that can be used all year long.

Here it's covered with fabric to match the bedroom quilt cover. The top edge is trimmed with a contrasting print in the same colors. Fill it with balls of yarn for a pretty and functional gift.

Materials: Mushroom basket; printed fabric; white glue; 3-inch-wide eyelet; 1-inch grosgrain ribbon.

Directions

Measure all sides of basket. When cutting the fabric for each section add a few inches, to compensate for irregularities.

When wrapping the outside edges clip the fabric where it wraps around at each end to compensate for the curves and tapers of the shape. Spread glue evenly over entire surface of the

basket. Attach fabric and press down. Overlap to the bottom and over the top edge.

Cut fabric and line inside walls in the same way. Extra fabric can extend onto bottom but not over the top.

Cut a piece to fit into the bottom and for the underside of the basket. Glue eyelet around outside top edge. Finish with 1-inch satin ribbon around top edge and tie with a bow.

Another design is created with a red and green berry print. The edge of the basket is trimmed with eyelet and green satin ribbon. It's used to hold Christmas napkins. This fabric is from Fabrications' International Printworks (see source list, page 160).

Soft fabric baskets

I've always found hundreds of uses for berry baskets. These pressed paper boxes sometimes hold tomatoes, grapes, or other foods. In my book *The Great Bazaar* (Delacorte Press) I show how to cover different sizes with vinyl wallcovering. When spray varnished, they look like porcelain. Use them as containers for gifts of food.

This time I've disguised the berry baskets with padding and moiré fabric and added some trimmings.

Since the items are small you'll need only a little fabric to cover them. Besides moiré, you could use elegant materials such as velvet, satin, lace, or brocade to make this a boutique item. The cost is minimal, but the results are great.

Materials: 2 berry baskets; small pieces of blue and rust color moiré fabric; quilt batting; 18 inches gold rickrack; 18 inches blue velvet braid; 1 yard each of white eyelet and lace; 12 inches of ½-inch-wide pink satin ribbon; 1½ yards of ½-inch white satin ribbon; piece of cardboard for handle and inside bottom; glue.

Directions

Cut a strip of quilt batting to wrap around outside of basket. Dot glue here and there and attach batting. Repeat inside (not on bottom).

Place basket in center of fabric. Draw all sides up and over top rim while creating gentle folds as you fit it around the basket. Tuck fabric inside so it completely covers.

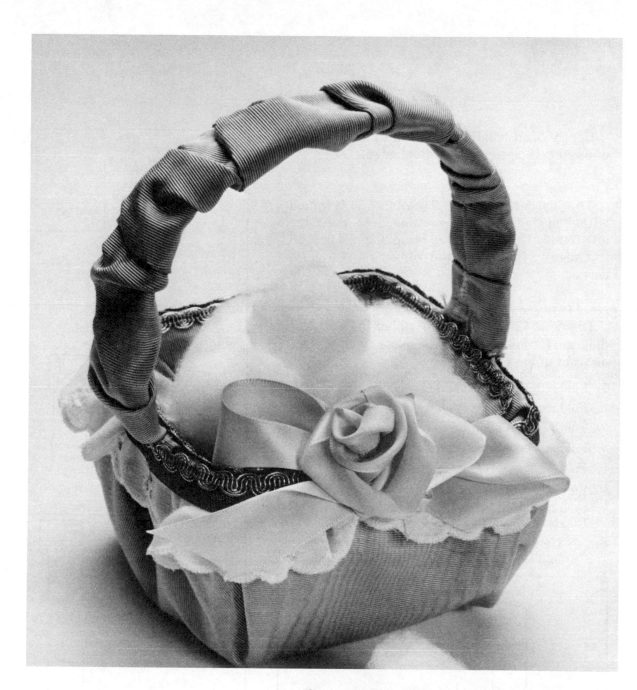

Cut a cardboard piece slightly smaller than inside bottom. Glue small piece of batting on cardboard and cover with fabric. Spread thin coat of glue on bottom of cardboard and press into bottom of basket, securing all fabric from sides.

Handle

Cut a piece of cardboard 1 × 10 inches. Cut a piece of the fabric 1½ × 15 inches. Glue a strip of batting to one side of cardboard. Place batting side down in center of fabric and turn ends up. Glue to cardboard ends.

Next spread glue over back of cardboard strip. Fold one side of fabric over, crinkling the fabric as you bunch it up and fit it over the batting. Fold other edge down to secure.

Gently bend handle and stitch to either inside of basket. Glue rickrack around edge.

Lace trim

The basket without a handle is trimmed with wide gathered lace stitched to the edge all around. The thin velvet braid is glued around top edge to finish off. Add ribbon roses to each corner.

Rose trim

Divide a 12-inch piece of ribbon in half. See diagram for folding into rose shape. Tack in place on front of basket.

1. Fold left end up at middle.
2. Fold right end over to left side.
3. Fold right end behind to right side.
4. Fold left end down.
5. Fold right end behind left side.
6. Fold left end up.
7. Fold right end behind right side.
   Repeat and continue to end of ribbon.
8. Hold ends of ribbon and pull left end gently through last fold to create rose shape.

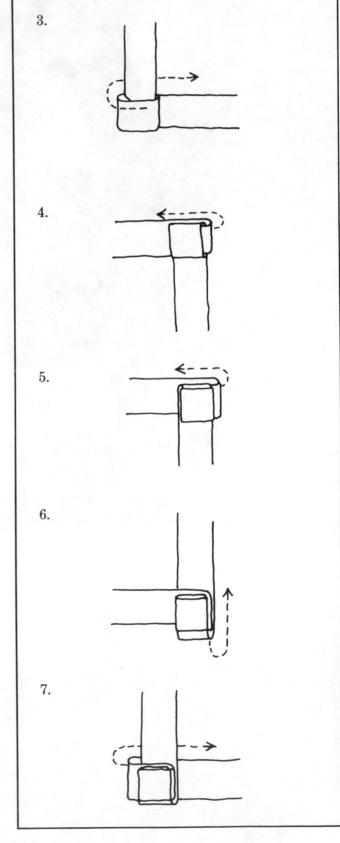

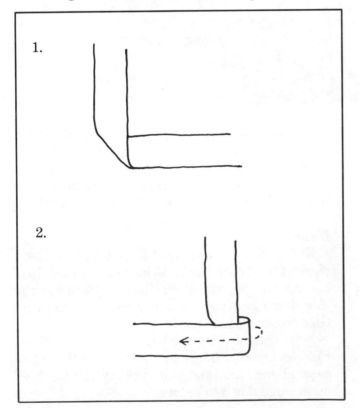

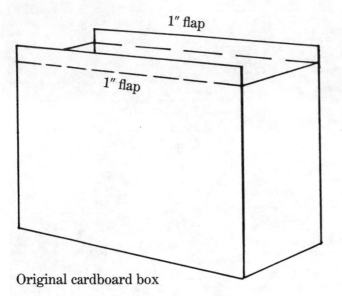

1" flap

1" flap

Original cardboard box

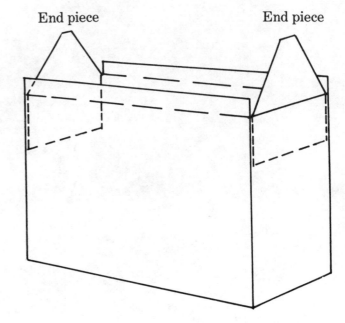

End piece

End piece

Would you believe this dollhouse combination toy box is made entirely from throwaway paper and corrugated boxes? The basic house is made from a sturdy liquor carton.

You can add window boxes, a welcome sign, flowers in a pot at the front door, front steps, molding, etc., to make this project as elaborate as you want.

Materials: Liquor carton; various kinds of wrapping paper or wallcovering; scraps of paper; craft knife; rubber cement; glue; scraps of cardboard; posterboard.

Directions

Trim flaps off evenly all around from liquor carton. Measure down 1 inch on all edges and draw a line at this mark. Cut off the 1-inch piece from short ends.

Use a craft knife to cut through 1 layer on long sides to score the cardboard. This will enable the roof pieces to fold out to open.

Cut 2 end pieces (see diagram) and glue them to the inside of the box ends (outside). Cut the chimney pieces and glue to outside of end pieces,

aligning bottom edge of chimney with top edge of box.

Cut out roof pieces A and B as per pattern.

Glue to scored 1-inch flaps on long sides of box. This will make the opening roof flaps.

Cut textured paper or wallcovering to cover all outside walls of house and chimney. (See page 151 for dry mounting with rubber cement.)

From cardboard or posterboard cut out 18 window shapes, $2\frac{1}{2} \times 3\frac{1}{2}$ inches.

1. Cover window shape with yellow patterned paper. Wrap around edges and glue to back of cardboard.
2. Cut window shades or curtains from blue printed paper and glue to top half of window.
3. Use pattern provided and cut window frame from thin posterboard. Glue solid color paper to frame. Glue frame over windows.
4. Cut a $2\frac{1}{2} \times 5$–inch door from cardboard and cover with paper. Cut out and glue frame in position around door edge.
5. Position and glue windows and doors on front and sides of box. The windows are set $1\frac{1}{2}$ inches up from bottom of house.

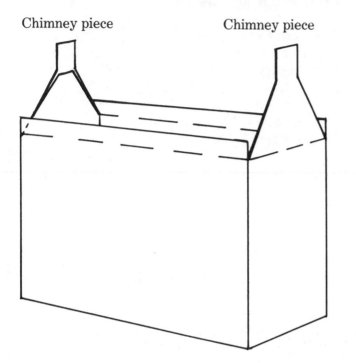

Chimney piece   Chimney piece

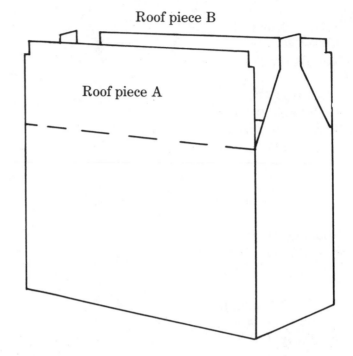

Roof piece B

Roof piece A

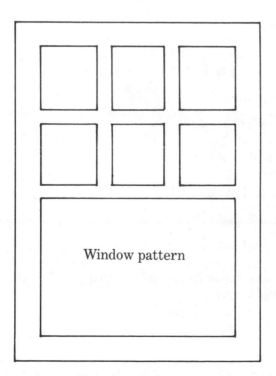

Window pattern

Mail-order sources

Art materials

Arthur Brown, Inc.
2 West 46th St.
New York, NY 10036

Charrette
31 Olympia Ave.
Woburn, MA 01801
(catalog $1)

Boxes and wood products

Houston Art and Frame Co.
P.O. Box 47164
Houston, TX 77027

O-P Craft Company
425 Warren St.
Sandusky, OH 44870
(catalog $1)

The Cracker Barrel
527 Narberth Ave.
Haddonfield, NJ 08033
(mushroom baskets)

Crochet and knitting patterns

Anne Lane Originals
P.O. Box 206
North Abington, MA 02351
(Christmas stockings)

The Crochet Works
1472 Auburn
Baker, OR 97814
(angels, snowflake ornaments—catalog 25¢)

Cross-stitch supplies

American Cross-Stitch
P.O. Box 4235
Parkersburg, WV 26101

Enterprise Art
2860 Roosevelt Blvd.
Clearwater, FL 33520

Wang's International Inc.
P.O. Box 16589
Memphis, TN 38186-0586
(Flexi-Hoop™)

Felt

Commonwealth Felt Company
211 Congress St.
Boston, MA 02110

Grid fabric

International Printworks
Fabrications
1740 Massachusetts Ave.
Cambridge, MA 02138

Needlecraft supplies

The Stitchery
Dept. 143
Wellesley, MA 02181

Stencil supplies

Whole Kit & Kaboodle Company
8 West 19th St.
New York, NY 10011
(catalog $1.50)

Have BETTER HOMES AND GARDENS® magazine delivered to your door. For information, write to: Mr. Robert Austin, P.O. Box 4536, Des Moines, IA 50336.